Manual of Knights Templar

Also from Westphalia Press

westphaliapress.org

The Idea of the Digital University

Masonic Tombstones and Masonic Secrets

Treasures of London

The History of Photography

L'Enfant and the Freemasons

Baronial Bedrooms

Making Trouble for Muslims

Material History and Ritual Objects

Paddle Your Own Canoe

Opportunity and Horatio Alger

Careers in the Face of Challenge

Bookplates of the Kings

Collecting American Presidential Autographs

Freemasonry in Old Buffalo

Original Cables from the Pearl Harbor Attack

Social Satire and the Modern Novel

The Essence of Harvard

The Genius of Freemasonry

A Definitive Commentary on Bookplates

James Martineau and Rebuilding Theology

No Bird Lacks Feathers

Earthworms, Horses, and Living Things

The Man Who Killed President Garfield

Anti-Masonry and the Murder of Morgan

Understanding Art

Homeopathy

Ancient Masonic Mysteries

Collecting Old Books

Masonic Secret Signs and Passwords

The Thomas Starr King Dispute

Earl Warren's Masonic Lodge

Lariats and Lassos

Mr. Garfield of Ohio

The Wisdom of Thomas Starr King

The French Foreign Legion

War in Syria

Naturism Comes to the United States

New Sources on Women and Freemasonry

Designing, Adapting, Strategizing in Online Education

Gunboat and Gun-runner

Meeting Minutes of Naval Lodge No. 4 F.A.A.M

Manual of Knights Templar

by Edward J. Newman

WESTPHALIA PRESS
An imprint of Policy Studies Organization

Westphalia Press
An imprint of Policy Studies Organization
1527 New Hampshire Ave., NW
Washington, D.C. 20036
info@ipsonet.org

ISBN-13: 978-1941472972
ISBN-10: 1941472974

Cover design by Taillefer Long at Illuminated Stories:
www.illuminatedstories.com

Daniel Gutierrez-Sandoval, Executive Director
PSO and Westphalia Press

Devin Proctor, Director of Media and Publications
PSO and Westphalia Press

Updated material and comments on this edition
can be found at the Westphalia Press website:
www.westphaliapress.org

MANUAL

OF

KNIGHTS TEMPLAR

ASYLUM CEREMONIES
AND TACTICS

—

MINNESOTA

1938

ERRATA

The following printing errors appear in the Manual of Asylum Ceremonies:

Page 52, Line 24, **"preparaory"** should be **"PREPARATORY."**

Page 88, starting of second paragraph should read:

"At page 99, line 18 of Ritual, when addressed, J. W. will arise, draw sword, salute, and after the word "Questions", Line 20, march diagonally to position in front of Commander, etc.

Page 89, third line from bottom of page should read:

"lines 12 and 13 on page of 124 of Ritual. Explanations"

Page 91, Line 12, "J. W." should read **"S. W."**

In Installation Service, wherever the word "Sir" appears at start of charges, it should be given as **"Sir Knight"** according to latest nomenclature of Grand Encampment.

Page 103—First line may be changed to read, **"The Knights, with or without uniforms, as the presiding Commander may order,"** will assemble in, etc.

(Kindly paste in Manual.)

PREFACE

To the KNIGHTS TEMPLAR
of Minnesota

At the 1935 Annual Conclave of the Grand Commandery, the recommendations of the Grand Commander with reference to preparing and presenting "to the Grand Commandery for adoption a work to be known as the 'Manual of Asylum Ceremonies and Tactics' which shall contain a detailed explanation of the floor work, tactics and sword movements to be used in conferring the various Orders, together with detailed tactics for opening in full form, for forming escorts and receiving Inspecting Officers and distinguished visitors, the use of which, when adopted, be made mandatory in all Constituent Commanderies," by the Board of Instructors was adopted, and the Board has endeavored to comply with such instructions.

It has been our desire to prepare a Manual which will fully cover every form of work or movement that may be conferred or performed in an Asylum, as distinguished from Drill or other Display Movements, and so far as possible, avoid duplications, but we find many movements that are similar, and in order that the Manual may contain instruction on all Asylum Movements, we have found some duplications necessary.

We have made liberal use of the Grand Encampment Drill Regulations, by permission of the Grand Master, especially with reference to the Manual of the Sword, School of the Officer, School of the Knight and the Squad and other subjects, believing that uniformity with the Grand Encampment Drill Regulations and Manual of Asylum Ceremonies is advisable and beneficial. It has also been our desire to consolidate or rewrite into this Manual all that believed to be of benefit as found in the various books that have been in use in this jurisdiction in the past, so that this Manual may be the only book necessary to be consulted in connection with Asylum Ceremonies. The task of research and compilation has not been an easy one, but if our efforts prove of value and benefit, we feel fully repaid for our work.

Courteously yours,

EDWARD J. NEWMAN, Chairman,
FRED G. WRIGHT, Secretary,
GEORGE F. DIX,
J. MERRITT FREEMAN,
FORREST F. SLYFIELD,
RICHARD JOHNSON,
BOARD OF INSTRUCTORS.

Approval

**The Grand Commandery, Knights Templar
of Minnesota.**

Office of

THE GRAND COMMANDER

St. Paul, Minn., June 22, 1938.

By the power and authority in me vested as Grand
Commander of the Grand Commandery of Knights
Templar of Minnesota, I hereby approve the final report of the Board of Instructors on the Manual of Asylum Ceremonies and Tactics, the compilation and preparation of which was authorized in 1935, partly approved in 1936 and fully approved in 1938, and approve
its publication in the form presented.

Jacob Ziegler.

Grand Commander

GENERAL INSTRUCTIONS

The Commander should not only be thoroughly conversant with his own duties, but should insist that each officer becomes proficient in the Asylum Ceremonies. To this end he should drill them from time to time until every movement is well understood. They should also be practiced in giving commands and estimating distances, combining in all things, practice with theory and study.

It is the right and duty of the Commander always to take command at drills, parades, schools of instruction, funerals, etc. This duty may be delegated to such other officer as the Commander may designate.

Officers on all duties, when under arms, draw and return swords at the proper time, without command.

When in command of a uniformed and armed body of Sir Knights, they will have their swords drawn, and as a rule will face the Sir Knights when giving a command.

The Senior Warden and Junior Warden in succession should be ready to promptly form the Commandery, and turn it over to the Captain General in due order for drill, parade, etc., also see that the Sir Knights keep their proper position and understand the orders given, animate and encourage them at drill, and generally to assist the Captain General as directed.

The Sword Bearer is the proper officer to pass the ballot box.

Before reporting alarms at door, the Warder should draw his sword and salute. In passing the Standard Guard he will pass in the rear of the Colors.

Sir Knights, when seated, at the command, Commandery, ATTENTION, will rise, without drawing swords, and remain standing until given further orders.

Except in electing officers, when written ballot is used, votes will be taken by show of hands, thus: "All in favor of the motion (or, adopting the resolution), will extend the sword arm. "Withdraw." "All opposed by the same sign." "Withdraw."

DEFINITIONS

About: A wheel or face of 180 degrees (a half circle).

Alignment: A straight line upon which several Sir Knights or Ranks are formed or are to be formed.

Base: The element on which a movement is regulated.

Cadence: The uniform time of step in marching or the succession of movements, in the sword manual:
Quick Time—120 movements per minute.
Double Time—180 movements per minute.
Common Time—90 movements per minute.
Sword Cadence at a halt executed in quick time.
Sword Cadence on the march executed in marching time.

Center: The middle point or element of a command.

Column: A formation in which the elements are placed one behind another·

Commander: The officer, junior officer or Sir Knight who is actually in command of the lines. The honorary title of the head of the Commandery is "Eminent Commander."

Company: A subdivision of a commandery; not less than two platoons.

Company Leader: An officer or junior officer of any grade, or Knight, in command of a company (twenty-four files so designated.)

Cover: To take position exactly in rear of another.

Deploy: To extend the front. In general to change from column to line, or from close to extended order.

Depth: The space from head to rear of any formation, including the leading and rear elements. The depth of a man is assumed to be 12 inches.

Distance: Space between elements in the direction of depth. (See Par. 187—G. E. D. R.)

Division: A sub-division of a commandery formed for asylum ceremonies. (see platoon). A sub-division of the grand parade of the Grand Encampment or of a Grand Commandery·

Drill: The exercises and evolutions taught in the asylum or on the drill field, and executed in the precise and formal manner prescribed.

Dress: Alignment to the right or left as in forming a rank.

Echelon: Elements placed one behind another; extending beyond and unmasking one another, either wholly or in part.

Element: A file, squad, section, platoon, company or larger body, forming a part of a still larger body (see unit).

Facing Distance: About 10 inches, i. e., the difference between the front of a Knight in ranks and his depth.

Field Officer: Officers of the grade of battallion commander and the commanders of higher units, excepting Marshal (General).

File: A Knight in rank. If in double rank includes the corresponding rear rank Knight. A line faced to the right (or left) is called a column of files.

File Closers: Officers or junior officers placed in rear of the line whose duty is to rectify mistakes and to command sub-divisions.

File Leader: The leading Knight whom the other Knights or files cover.

Flank: The right or left of a command in line or in column.

Formation: Arrangement of the Knights of a command. The placing of all fractions in their order in line or in column.

Front: The space in width occupied by a command or any element. The front of a Knight is 22 inches. Also the general direction toward which the command is moving.

Guide: One upon whom the command or Knight regulates the march.

Guidon: A small banner displaying the name and number of a Commandery or larger organization. (See Marker.)

Head: The leading element of a column.

Interval: Space between elements of the same line.

Junior Officers: All officers below the rank of Captain General (see officers).

Left in Front: A column formed to the left from line, or to the rear from front. (See Right in Front.)

Line: A formation in which the different elements are abreast of each other.

Marching Flank: The flank furthest from the pivot in turning or wheeling.

Marker: (See Guidon.)

Motion: Distinct movements in the Manual of the Sword.

Officers: The Captain General and all officers above that grade, and Past Commanders. (See Junior Officers.)

Pace: Thirty inches; the length of the full step in quick time.

Pivot: The Knight on the flank upon which the wheel or turn is made.

> **Fixed Pivot:**—The Knight on the pivot marks time and turns his body to conform to the front of the unit, gaining no ground during the execution of the movement.

> **Moving Pivot**—The Knight on the pivot moves on the arc of a circle the radius of which is 30 inches, and turns his body to conform to the front of the unit.

Platoon: A sub-division of a commandery, usually not less than 12 files formed for drill (see division).

Platoon Leader: An officer, or junior officer of any grade, or a Knight, in command of a platoon.

Ploy: To diminish front, as to pass from line to column.

Point of Rest: The point at which a formation begins.

Post: Official position or place of officers or Knights.

In Quarte: When the Sword Gripe is held, back of the hand down.

Rank: A line of Knights placed side by side; also the grade of an officer.

Right: The right extremity or element of a body of Knights. (contra, the left)

Right in Front: A column formed to the right from line. When the right of the line is on the right. A formation when the right of the line is in front. When the guide, in column of threes or sections, is on the left. When the file closers are on the right flank of the column.

Roster: A list of officers or knights for duty. The Roll of officers and Knights of a Commandery.

Section: Two sets of three abreast, in column or in line.

Squad: A small number of Knights for drill.

Sub-Division: The several parts into which a Commandery or larger body is divided, as threes, sections, platoons, etc.

In Tierce: When the sword gripe is held, back of the hand up.

Turn: A movement placing a rank at right angles to its former position, but executed by the Knights individually in succession.

Under Arms: Equipped with accoutrements, with sword drawn or in scabbard.

Unit: (See Element.)

Verify: To assure the correctness of a formation.

Wheel: A circular movement by which a rank is placed at right angles to its former position.

Wheeling Distance: A distance between subdivisions in column so that when wheeled into line the subdivisions will exactly join. Equal to the front of the subdivision less the depth of a Knight.

Wing: That portion of a Commandery, battalion, or larger body, from the center to the flank.

SALUTES

Officers will salute with sword or hand, according as the sword is drawn or in its scabbard. Upon addressing or being addressed, the Junior will always make the first salute, which will be acknowledged by the Senior. If the salute is with the sword, both come to CARRY simultaneously and stand at ATTENTION; or the Junior may stand at SALUTE while making a short report. They should always exchange salutes at the close of the conversation.

The Sovereign Master or Commander, if seated, does not arise to acknowledge a salute, and the High Priest or Prelate acknowledges salutes by bowing ceremoniously.

An officer should always have his sword drawn when giving a Command. (Ritual page 1.)

The Grand Master, Grand Commander, their Representatives and Past Grand Commanders are the only Sir Knights entitled to be received under an arch of steel.

Officers and Sir Knights, covered or uncovered, but not in formation, without swords or with swords in scabbard, salute with the hand salute, holding the hand to the chapeau or cap until the salute is acknowledged or the officer passed.

At no time, no place, or under any circumstances, is a sword drawn to acknowledge a salute already given.

When in ranks Sir Knights never uncover or salute except by command. Never salute and uncover at the same time.

An officer is "in formation," but never "in ranks."

A Sir Knight in ranks will not salute when directly addressed, but will come to attention if at rest or at ease.

If two commanderies or subdivisions meet, their Commanders will exchange salutes, both commands being at attention.

When passing in review an officer salutes, executing eyes right, and looks toward the reviewing officer when he is six paces from him, and returns to the carry and turns the head and eyes to the front when he has passed six paces beyond him.

Officers and Sir Knights, in replying to a question from the Commander or other superior officer, rise and salute. The title of the Commander or other superior officer should not be given with the salute.

The Prelate, when in uniform, salutes the same as other officers; if in robes, he salutes and acknowledges a salute by bowing ceremoniously.

ALARMS, Warder and Sentinel Duties

Alarms on doors, when done with sword, should be made with the flat side of the point of the blade rather than with the hilt.

The Sentinel should never permit any one to make an alarm on the door of the Asylum. He is at all times in full control of the door, and nobody should be allowed to open or close the door but himself. When a visitor or member of the Commandery desires to gain admission, the Sentinel himself should approach the door of the Asylum and give the required battery, always exercising care not to give the battery at a time during the conferring of an Order, that would disturb the ceremony. The same should apply to the spreading of the ballot or other important business. The battery being given, the Warder will arise, draw his sword, salute, and say:

Warder-Eminent Commander, there is an alarm.

Commander-Sir Knight Warder, attend to the alarm.

The Warder comes to carry swords and goes behind the Standards, to the door and gives the proper battery, and waits until the Sentinel opens the door, then ascertains the cause of the alarm as follows:

Warder: Sir Knight Sentinel, what is the cause of the alarm,

Sentinel-Sir Knight Warder, the alarm (then give cause of alarm.)

(It may be necessary for the Warder to go outside, if so, after ascertaining the cause of the alarm he will re-enter the Asylum and go to his station, passing behind the Standards, and report: The Sentinel closes the door.)

Warder-Eminent Commander, the alarm was caused by the Sir Knight Sentinel, modifying his report to suit the report made to him by the Sentinel. The Commander then instructs as the occasion demands.

The Sentinel should never give an alarm more then once for a particular occasion, especially when he knows that some important business or work is going on. The Warder is the only officer permitted to give the battery from the inside of the Asylum. He should also go to the door when anybody is to retire and make proper battery and see that the Sentinel opens and closes the door after a member, officer or unit passes in or out. If the movement, is to or through the preparation room door, the Warder will take entire charge of the door, no battery being given.

ORDERS, COMMANDS and SIGNALS

Officers and Sir Knights fix their attention at the first word of command, the first note of the bugle, or the first motion of the signal. A signal includes both the preparatory command and the command of execution; the movement commences as soon as the signal is understood, unless otherwise prescribed.

Commanders or leaders of subdivisions repeat orders, commands or signals, whenever such repetition is deemed necessary to insure prompt and correct execution.

Prescribed signals are limited to such as are essential as a substitute for the voice under conditions which render the voice inadequate.

In these regulations an order embraces instructions or directions given orally or in writing in terms suited to the particular occasion and not prescribed herein.

Orders are employed only when the commands prescribed herein do not sufficiently indicate the will of the Commander.

In these regulations a command is the will of the Commander expressed in the phraseology prescribed herein.

There are two kinds of commands.

The PREPARATORY command, such as **Forward,** indicates the movement that is to be executed·

The command of EXECUTION, such as **MARCH, HALT,** or **SWORDS,** causes the execution.

Preparatory commands are distinguished by **small black letters;** those of execution by **BLACK CAPITALS.**

Where it is not mentioned in the text who gives the commands prescribed, they are to be given by the Commander of the unit concerned.

The preparatory command should be given at such an interval of time before the command of execution as to admit of being properly understood; the command of execution should be given at the instant the movement is to commence.

The tone of command is animated, distinct, and of loudness proportioned to the number of men for whom it is intended.

Each preparatory command is enunciated distinctly, with a rising inflection at the end, and in such manner that the command of execution may be more energetic.

The command of execution is firm in tone and brief.

Oral commands are not habitually used for units larger than a battalion.

When giving commands to Sir Knights, it is usually best to face toward them.

Indifference in giving commands must be avoided, as it leads to laxity in execution. Commands should be given with spirit at all times.

To secure uniformity, all officers should practice giving commands.

An officer should always have his sword drawn when giving a command to Sir Knights under arms.

Bugle Signals

Bugle Signals are only used for ceremonies, and with large bodies for street parades and marches. (See Bugle Signals and Calls, D. R. par. 461.)

Whistle Signals

Attention to Orders. A short blast of the whistle. This signal is used on parades and marches when necessary to fix the attention of troops, or of their Commanders, or leaders, preparatory to giving commands, orders or signals.

13

Arm Signals

The following arm signals are prescribed. In making signals either arm may be used. In making arm signals, the sword may be held in the hand.

Forward, MARCH; Right oblique, MARCH; Left oblique, MARCH. Extend the arm vertically to its full extent and lower it to the front (right front), (left front) until horizontal; at the same time move in the indicated direction.

Quick Time, MARCH. Raise the right elbow to a position above and to the right of the right shoulder; extend the forearm to the left, right hand above the head. **HALT.** Carry the hand to the shoulder; thrust the hand upward and hold the arm vertically.

Double time, MARCH. Carry the hand to the shoulder; rapidly thrust the hand upward the full extent of the arm several times.

Change direction or **Column right (left), MARCH.** The hand on the side toward which change of direction is to be made is carried across the body to the opposite shoulder, forearm horizontal; then swing in a horizontal plane, arm extended pointing in the new direction.

SCHOOL of the OFFICER

The importance and responsibility of the officer in all Templar and military formations can not be over emphasized. He should be a model of promptness, dress, efficiency and appearance; should be devoted, enthusiastic and untiring, and to succeed must be a student and a gentleman.

Discipline and courtesy are as essential among Templars as with military men and must be maintained, yet the leader should not forget that his men are gentlemen, who out of ranks, are his peers.

Officers are described as those above and including the rank of Captain General and Past Commanders; those under that rank are classed as junior officers, the distinction being made to obtain the necessary parity with military formations and terms. However, in

'emplary no difference in class is recognized, except-
ıg in the measure of responsiblity; templar rank
sually being but temporary, and resulting often only
rom an accident of age or tenure.

The laws and decisions of the Grand Encampment
o not permit the wearing of the insignia of the U. S.
ɪrmy on the templar uniform, and it is also a techni-
al violation of the National Defense Act. In large as-
emblies and organizations some designation of temp-
ır military rank oftens seems necessary, but this need
an be met only by authority of the Grand Encamp-
ıent.

The recommendation for systematic training in a
chool for officers and junior officers is here renewed.
'he requirements should be regular attendance, strict
iscipline, and prompt commencement and dismissal.
ıfter the oral lesson the squad should be thoroughly
rilled in each movement. There should be the keenest
ttention and no talking in ranks. No faulty move-
ıent should ever be overlooked. The officers should
lternate as instructors, and all should be practiced in
·iving commands. If the Commander is not in charge
·e should appoint a chief instructor, preferably on per-
ıanent detail.

All drill commands to Templars under arms, mean-
ıg equipped with sword and accoutrements, are given
·ith sword drawn.

Unless otherwise directed officers omit the man-
al except the carry and order, parade rest, rest-on-
words, and kneelings; in rendering honors they exe-
ute the present, un-cover and re-cover; they draw and
eturn without command·

Officers may be in "formation", but are never in
ranks", unless temporarily so absorbed, when they
·ill drill and present like other Sir Knights. Whether
ı the station of officer junior officer, or Knight, by
ppointment or otherwise, a Knight Templar will al-
·ays conform with the honors and courtesies relating
o that grade.

Officers salute, by the officers present, or salute
words.

Officers or junior officers, commanding companies,
·latoons, a division or an escort, will use the salute

swords; at the command **PRESENT**, they will exe
cute the present and at **SWORDS**, will take the position
of salute swords.

Officers in ranks taking the place of Knights
and all other junior officers, execute the present sword
prescribed for Knights.

In double time, officers bring the sword across the
body at an angle of forty-five degrees, edge out and
about six inches in front of the breast, right hand for
ward, forearm horizontal, blade crossing opposite the
left shoulder, left hand steadying the scabbard (if no
hooked up), right arm swinging easily.

On drill or march the commanding officer goes
wherever his presence is necessary, but in ceremonies
every officer, junior officer and Knight must take the
position and post prescribed.

SCHOOL of the KNIGHT

Provision should be made for the proper instruc
tion of newly created Knights in essentials of facings
marching, wheeling and sword manual to preven
their falling into awkward or bad habits, as well as t
give grace and ease of movement. To this end the fol
lowing exercises are prepared.

Individual Drill, Without Swords

The drill should always commence promptly a
the appointed time. Punctuality, silence in ranks and
close attention during drill must always be insiste
upon.

The instructor explains briefly each movement
first executing it himself if practicable. He require
the Knights to take the proper positions unassisted an
does not touch them for the purpose of correcting
them, except when they are unable to correct them
selves. He avoids keeping them too long at the sam
movement, although each should be understood be
fore passing to another. He exacts by degrees the de
sired precision and uniformity. Drills should be in
fatigue uniform when possible and the sword manua
not taught until the Knights have acquired some pro
ficiency in the school of the officer, and the Knight.

For preliminary instruction a number of Knights, usually not exceeding three or four, are formed as a quad, in single rank facing to the front·

Position of the Knight, or Attention

Heels on the same line and as near each other as he conformation of the Knight permits.

Feet turned out equally and forming an angle of about 45 degrees.

Knees straight without stiffness.

Hips level and drawn back slightly; body erect and resting equally on hips; chest lifted and arched; shoulders square and falling equally.

Arms and hands hanging naturally; thumb along seam of the trousers.

Head erect and square to the front, chin slightly drawn in; eyes straight to the front. Weight of the body resting equally upon the heels and balls of the feet.

The Rests

Being at halt, the commands are:

1. FALL OUT, 2. REST, 3. AT EASE, 4. Stand at, 5. EASE, and 1. Parade, 2. REST.

At the command **fall out**, the Knights may leave the ranks but are required to remain in the immediate vicinity. They resume their former places, at attention, at the command **fall in.**

At the command **rest**, the Knight keeps one foot in place but is not required to preserve silence or immobility.

At the command **at ease**, the Knight keeps one foot in place and is required to preserve silence but not immobility.

Stand at Ease

1. Stand at, 2. EASE.

Being at order swords, at the command "EASE" carry the left foot twelve inches straight to the left, keeping the legs straight without stiffness, so that the weight of the body rests equally on both feet. At the same time incline the blade to the front by extending the right arm, without moving the point or changing the grasp on the hilt. Place the left hand behind the body, resting in the small of the back, palm to the rear, the attitude erect but not constrained. This secures dignified uniformity while resting.

1. Parade, 2. REST.

Carry the right foot 6 inches straight to the rear, feet at an angle of 45 dgrees, left knee slightly bent; clasp the hands, without constraint, in front of the center of the body, fingers joined, left hand uppermost, left thumb clasped by the thumb and forefinger of the right hand; preserve front, silence and steadiness of position.

To resume the attention:

1. Squad, 2. Atten-TION. (Given with accent on the last syllable,—TION.)

Eyes Right or Left

1. Eyes, 2. RIGHT (Left), 3. FRONT.

At the command right, turn the head to the right oblique (45 degrees), eyes fixed on the line of eyes of the Knights, in, or supposed to be in, the same rank. At the command front, turn the head and eyes smartly to the front.

Facings

To the flank: 1. Right (left), 2. FACE.

Raise slightly the left heel and right toe; face to the right (a one-fourth turn), turning on the right heel, assisted by a slight pressure on the ball of the left foot: (Two), place the left foot by the side of the right. Left, FACE, is executed on the left heel in the corresponding manner.

The right (left) half face, is executed similarly, facing 45 degrees, by command:

1. Half right (left), 2. FACE.

To FACE IN MARCHING and advance, turn on the ball of either foot and step off with the other foot in the new direction; to face in marching without gaining ground in the new direction, turn on the ball of either foot and mark time.

To the rear:

1. About, 2. FACE.

Carry the toe of the right foot about a half foot-length to the rear and slightly to the left of the left heel without changing the position of the left foot; (TWO), face to the rear (a one-half turn), turning to the right on the left heel and right toe, and place the right heel by the side of the left.

Salute With The Hand.
1. Hand, 2. SALUTE.

Raise the right hand smartly till tip of the forefinger touches the lower part of the headdress (if uncovered, the forehead) above the right eye, thumb and fingers extended and joined, palm to the left, forearm inclined at about 45 degrees, hand and wrist straight; at the same time look toward the person saluted; (TWO), drop the arm smartly by the side.

Steps and Marchings.

All steps and marchings executed from halt, except right step, begin with the left foot.

Hand Salute

The length of the full step in quick time is 30 inches, measured from heel to heel, and the cadence is at the rate of 120 steps per minute.

The length of the step in common time, is the same as in quick time; the cadence 90 steps per minute. Used in certain ceremonies, funeral, prelate's escort, etc., and for instruction.

The length of the full step in double time is 36 inches; the cadence is at the rate of 180 steps per minute.

The instructor, when necessary, indicates the cadence of the step by calling, **one, two, three, four, or, left, right,** the instant the left and right foot, respectively, should be planted.

All steps and marchings, and movements involving march are executed in quick time, unless the knights are marching in double time, or double time be added to the command; in the latter case double time is added to the preparatory command **1. Squad right, 2. Double time, 3. MARCH.** (Similarly for common time.) Quick time may be resumed from double time or common time. **1. Quick time, 2. MARCH.**

The command of execution for all movements while marching is given as either foot strikes the ground, except as otherwise prescribed; the movement commences when the following foot is planted.

Quick Time

Being at halt, to march forward in quick time. **1. Forward, 2. MARCH.**

At the command **forward,** shift the weight of the body to the right leg, left knee straight.

At the command **march,** move the left foot smartly straight forward 30 inches, sole near the ground, and plant it without shock; next, in like manner advance and plant the right foot; continue the march. The arms swing naturally.

Being at halt, or in march in quick time, to march in double time: **1. Double time, 2. MARCH.**

If at halt, at the first command shift the weight of the body to the right leg. At the command **MARCH,** raise the forearm, fingers closed, back of the hands out to a horizontal position along the waist line; take up an easy run with the step and cadence of double time, allowing a natural swinging motion of the arms.

In marching in quick time, at the command **MARCH,** given as either foot strikes the ground, take one step in quick time, and then step off in double time.

To resume the quick time: **1. Quick time, 2. MARCH.**

At the command **MARCH,** given as either foot strikes the ground, advance and plant the other foot in double time; resume the quick time, dropping the hands by the sides.

To Mark Time

Being in march: 1. Mark Time, 2. MARCH.

At the command **march,** given as either foot strikes the ground; advance and plant the other foot; bring up the foot in rear and continue the cadence by alternately raising each foot about two inches and planting it on line with the other.

Being at halt, at the command **march,** raise and plant first the left foot and then the right, as described above.

Any movement may be executed from **mark time.**

The Half Step

1. Half Step, 2. MARCH.

Take steps of 15 inches in quick time, 18 inches in double time.

Forward, half step, halt and mark time, may be executed one from the other in quick or double time.

To resume the full step from half step or mark time: **1. Forward, 2. MARCH.**

Side Step

Being at halt or mark time: **1. Right (left) step, 2. MARCH.**

Carry and plant the right foot 10 inches to the right; bring the left foot beside it and continue the movement in the cadence of quick time.

The side step is used for short distances only and is not executed in double time.

NOTE—The Command **halt** is given when the feet are together; take another step, then halt.

Back Step

Being at halt or mark time: **1. Backward, 2 MARCH.**

Take steps of 15 inches straight to the rear.

The back step is used for short distances only and is not executed in double time.

To Halt

To arrest the march in quick time or double time:
1. Squad, 2. HALT.

At the command **halt**, given as either foot strikes the ground, plant the other foot as in marching; raise and place the first foot by the side of the other. If in double time, drop the hands by the side.

To March By The Flank

Being in march: 1. By the right (left) flank, 2. MARCH.

At the command **march**, given as the right foot strikes the ground, advance and plant the left foot, then face to the right in marching and step off in the new direction with the right foot. Execute by the left flank by inverse commands and means. (The right and left face in marching.)

To March To The Rear

Being in march: 1. To the rear, 2. MARCH.

At the command **march**, given as the right foot strikes the ground, advance and plant the left foot; turn to the right about on the balls of both feet and immediately step off with the left foot.

If marching in double time, turn to the right about, taking four steps in place, keeping the cadence, and then step off with the left foot.

Change Step

Being in march: 1. Change step, 2. MARCH·

At the command **march**, given as the right (left) foot strikes the ground, advance and plant the left foot; plant the toe of the right foot near the heel of the left and step off with the left foot, both movements being executed in one count.

To Oblique March

The instructor causes the squad to face half right or half left, points out to the Knights their relative positions and explains that these are to be maintained in the oblique march: 1. **Right (left) oblique**, 2. **MARCH.**

Each Knight steps off in a direction 45 degrees to the right of his original front. He preserves his relative position, keeping his shoulders parallel to those of the guide (The Knight on the right (or left) front of the line or column), and so regulates his steps that the ranks remain parallel to their original front.

At the command halt, the Knights halt, faced to the front.

The command halt should be given on the left foot when halting from a right oblique, and on the right foot when halting from a left oblique.

To resume the original direction: 1. Forward, 2. MARCH.

The Knights half face to the left in marching and then move straight to the front.

If at a half step or mark time while obliquing, the oblique march is resumed by the commands: 1. Oblique, 2, MARCH.

The Route Step

1. Route step, 2. MARCH.

At the command march, the Knights lengthen or shorten the step at will, so that it will break the cadence, and are not required to preserve silence nor keep step. The ranks cover and preserve distance. The swords, if not in scabbards, carried at will. (To be given in crossing bridges or at funerals where the distance to the cemetery is great.) To resume the cadence, step and silence: 1. Squad, 2. ATTENTION.

SCHOOL of the SQUAD

To Align the Squad.

1. Squad, 2. FALL IN.

At the command **fall in**, the tallest Knight takes position where the right is to rest, facing to the right. The Knights fall in quickly in rear, at a distance of ten inches, according to height. At the command: **1. Left, 2. FACE**, they face to the left into line.

Alignments

The instructor first teaches the Knights to align themselves man by man; to this end he advances the two Knights on the right, three or more paces, and having aligned them, commands: **1. By file, right (left), 2. DRESS, 3. FRONT.**

At the command **dress**, the Knights move up successively in quick time, shortening the last step, so as to be about six inches behind the alignment which must never be passed; each Knight then executes **eyes right**, and moves on the line taking steps of two or three inches, places his right arm lightly against the left arm of the Knight on his right, so that his eyes and shoulders are in line with those of the Knights on his right, shoulders square to the front.

At the command **front**, given when the ranks are aligned, the Knights turn their heads and eyes smartly to the front.

The Knights having learned to align themselves man by man, the instructor next aligns them by the command: **1. Right (left), 2. DRESS, 3. FRONT.**

The base having been established, at the command **dress**, the entire rank moves forward and dresses up to the line as previously explained.

The instructor verifies the alignment from the right flank and orders up or back such men as may be in rear, or in advance of the line; only the men designated move.

At the command **front**, given when the rank is aligned, each man, except the base file executes **eyes right (or left)**.

Whenever the position of the base file or files necessitates a considerable movement by the squad, such movement will be executed by marching to the front or oblique, to the flank or backwards, as the case may be, without other command.

Alignments to the rear are executed on the same principles, the Knights stepping back a little beyond the line, and then dressing up, by steps of two or three inches. The commands are: 1. By file, right (left), backward, 2. DRESS, 3. FRONT, or 1. Right backward, 2. DRESS, 3. FRONT.

To March in Line

The Knights being correctly aligned, the instructor places a well instructed Knight on the side on which the guide is to be, and commands: 1. Forward, 2. MARCH.

At the command **march**, the Knights step off smartly with the left foot, the Knight acting as guide marching straight to the front.

The instructor observes, in marching in line, that the Knights touch lightly the elbow toward the side of the guide; that they open neither arm; that they yield to pressure coming from the side of the guide, and resist pressure coming from the opposite direction; that shortening or lengthening the step, they gradually recover the alignment and touch of the elbow, if lost, and that they keep the head direct to the front, no matter on which side the guide may be.

The instructor impresses upon the Knights that the alignment can only be preserved in marching, by the uniformity of the step, both in length and swiftness, by the touch of the elbow, and the maintenance of the shoulders square with the line of direction.

To March By the Flank

Being at halt, the instructor commands: 1. **Right** (left), 2. FACE, 3. Forward, 4. MARCH.

If in march, the instructor commands: 1. **By the right (left) flank, 2. MARCH.**

At the command **march**, given as the right foot strikes the ground, advance and plant the left foot, then turn to the right in marching and step off in the new direction with the right foot.

In the march by the flank the Knights cover each other, and keep to facing distance, that is, to such distance that in forming line, the elbows will touch.

A rank faced to the right or left is called a column of files. To halt the column of files, the instructor commands: 1.Squad, 2. HALT, and to face it to the front, 1. Left (right), 2. FACE.

Marching in column of files to march in line, the instructor commands: 1. By the right (left) flank, 2. MARCH.

To Change Direction in Column of Files

Being in march, the instructor commands: 1. Column right (left), or, 1. Column half right (left), 2. MARCH.

At the command **march**, the leading file turns to the right, or half right, on a moving pivot (with radius reduced), followed by the other files, who turn on the same ground.

To Oblique

Being well drilled in the principles of the direct march, the squad is taught to march obliquely. Marching in line, the instructor commands: 1. **Right (left) oblique**, 2. **MARCH**.

At the command **march**, each Knight makes a half face to the right, and then marches straight in the new direction. The Knights no longer touch elbows, but preserve the line of the rank parallel to its former position by the eye only, glancing along the shoulders of the nearest files, toward the side to which they are obliquing, and regulating their steps so that the shoulders are about six inches behind the shoulders of the Knights on that side, and that the heads conceal the heads of the other Knights in the rank. The Knights all preserve the same length of step, and the same degree of obliquity.

To resume the original direction, the instructor commands: 1. Forward, 2. MARCH.

At the command **march**, each Knight makes a half face to the left in marching, and then moves straight to the front. If the squad be at a halt, the Knights half face to the right, at the command **right oblique**, and step off at the command **march**.

Wheelings

Wheelings are of two kinds; on either a fixed or moving pivot.

To Wheel on a Fixed Pivot

1. In circle, 2. Left (right) wheel, 3. MARCH.

The Knight on the extreme right takes the full step and looks toward the pivot. All keep touch of elbows toward the pivot, head and eyes turned (eyes right) toward the marching flank, regulating the length of step accordingly. Thus continue until halted.

The **fixed pivot** is used in wheeling from line into column, or from column into line, the pivot Knight marking time in his place and turning to conform to the marching flank.

A wheel on a moving pivot, used in changing direction in marching, is made in the same manner, except that the pivot Knight takes a short step thus gaining ground forward, describing the circle with radius of 30 inches, regulating the length of his step to correspond with the marching flank.

The **moving pivot** is used in changing direction of column, and in some successive formations, the pivot Knight describing a circle the radius of which is always 30 inches.

MANUAL of the COLOR

At the carry, the heel (foot) of the pike (staff), rests in the socket of the sling; the right hand grasps the pike at the height of the shoulder.

At the order the heel of the pike rests on the ground near the right toe, the right hand holding the pike in a vertical position.

At parade rest the heel of the pike is on the ground as at the order; the pike is held with both hands in front of the center of the body, left hand uppermost.

The order is resumed at the command, **attention.**

The left hand assists the right hand when necessary, but when not assisting, should be at the left side.

The carry is the habitual position when on the march.

The order and parade rest are executed with the Commandery.

The **color salute**: Being at a carry, slip the right hand up the pike to the height of the eye, then lower the pike by straightening the arm to the front.

MANUAL of the SWORD

Only such sword movements as are most commonly used in the Asylum are included herein. For more detailed movements and diagrams of same, consult the Grand Encampment Drill Regulations.

Newly created Knights should at once be taught marching, drill and sword manual. Ease and grace can only be acquired by frequent exercise. Attention to minor details is essential in order to avoid the forming of awkward habits or taking incorrect positions. Carry the sword with a flexible wrist and without grasping the gripe tightly. The gripe should be held, at position of carry, by the thumb and forefinger, as if holding a pen, and covering about two-thirds of the gripe below the guard. Each command is divided into motions of one-half of a second, which should, at first, be explained and executed separately without reference to cadence. On the march the cadence corresponds with the step. The manual may first be taught by calling the numbers of motions, the command being prefaced by the words "By the numbers," No. ONE being executed at the command **swords**, or other command of execution, then TWO, THREE, etc., until the command "without the numbers," or until a command is given not in the sword manual. When on march if the swords are drawn and not at a carry, the Knights will, at the command **halt**, come to Carry Swords. without command. If in scabbard the left hand steadies same. While marching the hands may be allowed to swing forward and back three or four inches for the sake of ease and grace of carriage.

NOTE—With sword drawn or in scabbard, if desired, scabbard may be hooked up, uniformity being maintained. "Hooked up" means hanging by the front upper ring. If hooked up the scabbard must be unhooked before executing draw or return swords.

The sword consists of the hilt and the blade.

The hilt is divided into the gripe and the guard.

The gripe is the handle grasped by the hand.

The guard is the cross piece between the gripe and the blade.

The blade is divided into the edge, back, sides and point.

The edge and back are determined by the hilt.

The right and left sides of the blade and gripe are the right and left sides in the position of carry swords.

The scabbard is the receptacle of the sword; the opening of same, its mouth.

The hand is in tierce, when it holds the gripe, with back of hand up, and in quarte, when it holds the gripe with back of hand down.

Unless the formation is in open ranks, the Knights under instruction should take intervals.

Being in line at a halt with swords in scabbards:

Draw Swords   Draw Swords   Carry Swords
First Motion   Second Motion

1. Sir Knights, 2. Draw, 3. SWORDS.

At the command DRAW, grasp the scabbard with

the left hand, near its mouth, incline the hilt a little forward, seize the gripe with the right hand, and draw the blade until the right forearm is horizontal, back of hand against the breast.   SWORDS, draw the sword quickly raising the arm to its full length, at an angle of about 45 degrees, the sword in a straight line with the arm, edge down, extending in the same direction as the right foot.   (TWO) Bring the back of the blade against the shoulder, the blade vertical, back of the gripe to the rear, the arm nearly straight down, the thumb and forefinger embracing the gripe, the thumb against the thigh, the other fingers extended and joined in the rear of the gripe. This is the position of Carry Swords. From this position all movements of the sword manual begin, unless otherwise provided.

In all marching movements, except route march, at the command HALT, unless otherwise provided, the sword, if drawn, will be brought to the carry without command.

Sword Intervals
From the Right

1. From the right take sword intervals, 2. MARCH·

At the first command, all the Knights except the one on the right, who remains at Carry Swords, execute EYES RIGHT, raise the right hand in front of and as high as the right shoulder, the back of the hand to the front, and drop the sword blade horizontally to the right, edge up. MARCH, all the Knights except the right file, execute left step. As soon as each Knight has gained an interval so that the point of his sword will clear the left arm of the knight on his right, he halts, executes FRONT, and resumes Carry Sword.

NOTE — This movement intended only as preparatory to Par. 116 to 135, G. E. Drill Regulations.

1. From the left take sword intervals, 2. MARCH.

Is executed as above, except that the eyes are turned to the left, the right hand is carried across the body and touches the left arm, the right forearm horizontal, the sword extended in prolongation thereof, edge down.

Sword Intervals From the Left

1. On the right (left) close intervals, 2. MARCH·

The Knight on the right (left) stands fast, the others face him and march forward halting successively when the interval is closed, and facing to the front.

1. Present, 2. SWORDS.

Raise and carry the sword to the front, cross hilt as high as the chin and six inches in front of the neck, edge to the left, point six inches farther to the front than the cross hilt thumb extended on the back of the gripe, wrist straight, all fingers grasping the gripe.

1. Carry, 2. SWORDS.

Resume the carry in one motion, without throwing the right hand to the front, or the point to the rear.

Present Swords

1. Salute, 2. SWORDS.

Execute present swords (TWO)

Salute Swords Officers Present

Drop the point of the sword, edge to the left about fifteen inches in front of and in prolongation of the right

31

foot, arm hanging naturally, the elbow close to the body, the back of the hand down.

1. Carry, 2. SWORDS

Resume the position of carry swords.

The SALUTE SWORDS, is the present swords, used by officers. If not in ranks they will at the command PRESENT, execute present swords, and at the command SWORDS, execute the second motion of salute swords. Junior officers execute the present unless otherwise prescribed.

1. Order, 2. SWORDS.

Drop the sword point to the ground, blade inclined to the rear, back of blade to the front (TWO) Bring the blade to a vertical position against the right toe, and place the hand on top of the hilt, three fingers in front of the gripe, thumb and little finger in the rear, elbow close to the body.

1. Carry, 2. SWORDS.

Resume the position of carry swords, in one motion.

1. Support, 2. SWORDS. Bring the sword to the position of present (TWO)

First Motion   Order Swords
Order Swords

Carry the sword vertically to the left side, lowering the right hand until the forearm is horizontal, edge of the sword to the front the right hand firmly grasping the gripe about three inches below the guard, at the same time grasp the right foream near the elbow with the left hand, the left forearm along and in front of the right forearm, the thumb of the left hand over and supported by the right forearm near the elbow, fingers of the left hand extended and joined, the guard resting on the left arm near its elbow, the blade vertical, edge to the front.

1. Carry, 2. SWORDS.

Bring the sword to the position of present, at the same time drop the left hand by the side. (TWO) Bring the sword to the carry.

1. Swords, 2. PORT.

Seize the blade in front of the right shoulder with the fingers and thumb of the left hand, thumb to the rear, the left elbow close to the body. (TWO) With the left hand bring the sword diagonally across and about one inch in front of the body edge down, the left hand at the height of the left shoulder, the thumb extended along the blade, the fingers closed, back of the hand down, the right hand grasping the hilt and nearly in front of the right hip.

Support Swords

Swords Port

1. Carry, 2. SWORDS.

Bring the sword to the carry with both hands, the left hand as high as the right shoulder, pressing the blade to its place, the fingers and thumb extended and joined in front of the blade, the elbow near the body. (TWO) Drop the left hand to the side.

1. Arm Rest, 2. SWORDS.

Carry the hands in front of the center of the body, the arms nearly extended; clasp the hands the left over the right, the blade resting along the right forearm, the right hand retaining the same position on the gripe as at the carry.

Carry from Port
First Motion

Arm Rest-Swords

1. Carry, 2. SWORDS.

Resume the carry in one motion.

33

1. Shoulder, 2. SWORDS.

Raise the right hand in front of the armpit and place the flat of the sword blade on the right shoulder, the edge to the left, the elbow close to the body, the point of the sword obliquely to the left, and in the rear, clearing the chapeau.

1. Carry, 2. SWORDS.

Resume the position of carry swords.

1. Reverse, 2. SWORDS.

Drop the blade forward and down until it is directed towards a point about one pace in front of the right foot, at the same time allow the fingers to grasp the lower part of the gripe, and move the hand forward about twelve inches. (TWO) Carry the sword by a wrist movement so that the blade will swing to the rear, the point downward at an angle of about 45 degrees, the edge up. As the sword swings into position under the right arm pit, bring the hand in front of the right arm pit and grasp the gripe with the thumb and forefinger of the right hand, the other fingers successively curved, resting the blade between the right arm and the right side. The end of the hilt remains about nine inches in front of the right shoulder.

To resume the carry: 1. Carry, 2. SWORDS.

Bring the sword to the first position of reverse. (TWO) Resume the position of carry swords.

On long marches the corresponding position of left reverse may be taken.

Shoulder Swords

Reverse Swords First Motion

Reverse Swords

34

1. Left reverse, 2. SWORDS.

Extend the right hand to the first position of reverse. (TWO) With the right hand swing the sword to the position of left reverse. (THREE) Seize the gripe with the left hand and drop the right hand to the side.

1. Carry, 2. SWORDS.

Seize the gripe with the right hand and drop the left hand to the side. (TWO) Carry the sword to the first position of reverse swords. (THREE) Resume the position of carry swords.

1. Parade, 2. REST.

Being at the carry or order swords.

Drop (carry) the sword point to the ground in front of the center of the body on a line with the left toe, edge to the right, the palm of the right hand resting on the end of the hilt; the thumb and fingers extended and joined against the gripe, and left hand clasped over the right; at the same time carry the right foot six inches straight to the rear, the left knee slightly bent, the body erect.

Parade Rest

Attention
From Parade Rest

1. Squad, ATTENTION, 2. CARRY (order), 3. SWORDS.

At the command ATTENTION, bring the right foot to the side of the left; drop the left hand to the side, and carry the hilt to the right side, leaving the point undisturbed. At the command SWORDS, resume the position of carry (order) swords in one motion.

1. Inspection, 2. SWORDS.

Execute present swords, and turn the wrist to show both sides of the blade, resuming the carry when the inspector has passed.

1. Invert, 2. SWORDS.

Drop the point of the sword directly forward about fifteen inches, grasping the blade (about nine inches from the guard) with the left hand palm to the front. (TWO) Release the gripe with the right hand and invert the sword with the left hand to a position about four inches in front of the center of the body, blade vertical, edge to the right, guard at the height of the chin, grasp the blade with the right hand at the height of the belt.

Invert Swords
First Motion

Invert Swords

1. Carry, 2. SWORDS.

Release the right hand and swing the point of the sword forward and upward, at the same time lower the hilt to the right side and grasp it with the right hand (first position of the invert.) (TWO) Place the sword in the position of carry, the left hand at the right shoulder, turning the hand. (THREE) Drop the left hand to the side.

NOTE—Invert swords is used for ceremonial purposes, for devotions, as in church service during prayer in lieu of present swords.

1. Guide, 2. SWORDS.

Bring the sword vertically in front of the center of the body, the right hand as high as the neck and six inches in front of it, back of the gripe to the right at the same time clasp the left hand over the right, elbows close to the body.

To return to the carry: 1. Carry, 2. SWORDS.

Guide
Swords

36

Resume the position of CARRY SWORDS in one motion.

NOTE—Upon taking post on the line, as in successive formation in battalion drill, guides will take this position without command, returning to the carry at the command GUIDES POST.

1. Sir Knights, 2. Return, 3. SWORDS.

At the command RETURN, seize the scabbard near the mouth with the left hand, inclining it a little forward and keeping the right hand near the body, drop the sword blade forward and to the left so that the point is about six inches from the floor and pointing to a line which is a prolongation of the left foot. Move the sword hand to the left, then raise the hand, drawing the sword blade between the first two fingers of the left hand. Insert the point of the blade in the mouth of the scabbard, edge to the front, assisted by the thumb and fingers of the left hand, eyes to the front, thrust the blade into the scabbard until the right forearm is horizontal (first motion of draw). (SWORDS) Return the blade smartly and drop the hands to the sides.

Return Swords
First Motion

NOTE—In inserting the point avoid turning the scabbard to meet the sword.

1. Secure, 2. SWORDS.

Seize the scabbard with the left hand, palm to the front, the thumb to the left, the arm extended. (TWO) Raise the scabbard, bring the left hand in front, nearly as high as the belt and a little to the left of the belt clasp, the scabbard resting along the left forearm, the back of the hand down, the guard at the hollow of the elbow. (Executed only when swords are in scabbard.)

Secure Swords

37

1. Drop, 2. SWORDS.

Lower the scabbard to its place, and detach the hand.

NOTE—Only to be used by officers, on ceremonies, and in double time.

Position of Sword at Double Time, in Ranks.

1. Double time, 2. MARCH.

At the first command take the position of **Shoulder Swords,** left hand steadying the scabbard, thumb in front. (If swords are in scabbard take the position of **Secure Swords.**) At the command **March** take the double time, at the command, **Quick Time,** resume the carry.

This rule is general in all commands for double time.

MANUAL OF THE SWORD. (Ritual)

The following sword or asylum movements are those in force in the Grand Encampment at the present time as set out in the Grand Encampmnt Drill Regulations and Amendments thereto, and as such were adopted by the Grand Commandery of this State, and are mandatory, for use where they apply.

To form lines at open ranks for the reception of a grand officer, or to communicate, the line should be moved forward to the position which the front rank will ccupy. Ranks will then be opened, Par. 191 of G. E. Drill Regulations.

To form two divisions facing inward:

Being at open ranks at Halt:

1. Form two divisions, 2. Files, 3. COVER, 4. Front rank, 5. About, 6. FACE.

At the command COVER, the rear rank files take two right steps and become the first division. At the command FACE, the front rank faces about and becomes the second division, and the officers and guides will take position as follows: the right guide (S. W.) will execute about face, march forward one pace beyond the line of the first division, halt, face about and dress into line; the left guide (J. W.) will step forward one pace, face right in marching, continue forward, halt, face right and dress into line of the second division; the interior guides will face left, march forward and in a similar manner take position number two on the left flank of the first division and number three on the right flank of the second division; the platoon leaders will face right, march forward and take position, the first (G.) on the right of the first division and the second (C. G.) on the left of the second division; the Commander then takes position two paces to the right and midway between and facing the lines.

To reform line, the Commander commands:

1. Reform line, 2. Second division, 3. About, 4. FACE, 5. Close ranks, 6. MARCH.

At the command, REFORM LINE, the officers and guides proceed to their posts in line. At the command, FACE, the second division executes about face and at the command, MARCH, the ranks are closed.

1. GUARD.

Turn the left foot square to the left, turning on the left heel, and plant the right foot firmly about eighteen inches to the front, feet at right angles, the weight resting principally on the right foot, the shoulders oblique to the front, head and eyes square to the front. At the same time raise the sword hand on a line with lower part of the belt and about two inches from it, the guard three or four inches to the right of the belt clasp. Drop the sword diagonally to the left, the blade about 18 inches in front of the left shoulder, edge to the front, thumb on back or gripe. The sword held without constraint.

On Guard

1. Carry, 2. SWORDS.

Resume the position of attention at carry swords.

Cuts or Parries

After the Commander has given orders to one division to communicate to another division, a certain word, he will command:

1. GUARD, 2. GIVE CUTS: The cuts may be given without further commands, or the Commander may count as follows:

Parry One—Cross Swords

1. Parry, 2. ONE.
(Regardless as to whether the Commander counts, the following explanations govern the movements.)

Raise and extend the arm, back of hand to the left and up, without changing the grasp, wrist as high as the head, the edge of the sword up, the blade in prolongation of the forearm, and engage the sword of the Knight opposite.

1. Parry, 2. TWO.

Disengage the sword and describe a circular movement toward the rear and right, back of hand down, edge of sword down, the hand on a line with the head, and engage the opposite sword on the right side, crossing the blades as before.

1. Parry, 2. THREE.

Disengage the sword and describe a circular movement toward the left and downward, engage the opposite sword on the left side, the point of the sword near the ground, the edge upward, the back of the hand to the left, and cross blades.

Parry Three

1. Parry, 2. FOUR. Come directly to the position of PARRY ONE.

The parries may be taught by numbers, but when a commandery is well instructed they may be given, one division to another, by calling the number of the parry required as follows: First Division_____to the Second Division_____. As previously stated, the cuts may also be given without counting.

After each word is communicated, the position of on guard and carry swords will be resumed as follows:

1. Carry, 2. SWORDS. At the first command, come to the position of on guard and at the command swords, bring the right foot back to the original line and resume the carry.

1. Wield, 2. SWORDS.

Raise the sword to the second position of draw swords. Wield the sword four times in a circular motion to the left, stopping at the first position of wield swords.

1. Carry, 2. SWORDS.

Resume the position of carry swords.

To Form Arch of Steel.

NOTE—The following with reference to forming arch of steel has no application to forming the arch over the triangle in the conferring of the Order of the Temple. Has no application at line 8, page 123 of Ritual.

The commandery being formed in two lines, facing inward, and about three paces apart, at carry swords, the command will be given:

1. Form arch of steel, 2. Cross, 3. SWORDS.

(ONE) Execute present swords. (TWO) Advance the right foot and take the position of Parry One.

1. Carry, 2. SWORDS.

Bring the sword to the position of present and replace the feet. (TWO) Resume the position of carry swords.

1. REST on, 2. SWORDS. (From Kneel at Parade Rest.)

Incline the head forward, the eyes fixed on the point of the sword.

To resume attention.

1. Sir Knights, 2. ATTENTION.

At SIR KNIGHTS, raise the head.

The Rest on Swords can also be executed from the parade rest without kneeling.

1. Charge, 2. SWORDS.

NOTE—The following explanation of "Charge" has no application at Line 5, page 123 of Ritual.

Turn on the left heel, placing the toe square to the left; at the same time plant the right foot forward with a slight shock about eighteen inches, the feet being at right angles, the weight of the body resting on the right foot. At the time of planting the feet extend the arm to its full length, at

Charge Swords

the height of the shoulder, back of the hand down, the blade in prolongation of the arm, and pointed at the opponent's breast.

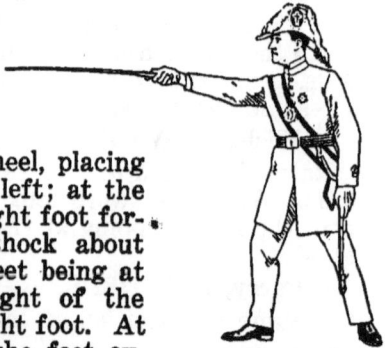

1. Carry, 2. SWORDS.

Resume the position of attention at carry swords.

1. Un- 2. COVER.

At the command COVER, take the chapeau by the front piece with the left hand. (TWO) Raise the chapeau from the head and place it on the right shoulder, slightly to the front, holding it in that position with the left hand.

1. Re- 2. COVER.

Replace the chapeau on the head. (TWO) Drop the hand to the side.

Un-cover

NOTE—Uncover is never executed unless the swords are sheathed, at an order or (with the right hand,) when at a secure.

1. Sir Knights, 2. KNEEL. (Swords sheathed)

Carry the left foot about twenty-four inches to the rear. (TWO) Kneel on the left knee, the body and left thigh erect, the right leg below the knee nearly vertical, the right hand hanging at the side.

The triangle guard kneel, from order swords, same as above, except as to the right hand, which rests on the top of the sword hilt.

1. Deposit, 2. CHAPEAU. (From uncover, kneeling.)

Deposit
Chapeaux

At the second command, place the chapeau on the ground to the left of the right foot, feathers to the left, peak pointing toward the body. The cap is placed with the crown down. (TWO) Resume position of kneel.

After communication:

1. Secure, 2. Chapeau, 3. RECOVER, 4. Sir Knights, 5. ARISE.

At the second command grasp the visor of the chapeau with the left hand, place it on the right shoulder. (THREE) Replace the chapeau on the head and drop the hand. (FIVE) All rise bringing left feet forward into line.

Kneel
Rest on
Swords

NOTE—The uncover should be made after kneeling and before rising.

After devotion:

1. RECOVER, 2. Sir Knights, 3. ARISE.

(One) Replace the chapeau on the head and drop the hand to the side.

(THREE) All rise bringing left feet forward into line.

COMMANDERY

Full Form Opening

(All officers, Commander to Warder inclusive, except the Prelate (when in robes) who bows ceremoniously, will use the sword salute as per Par. 90, G. E. Drill Regulations, The Commander may use either Hand or Sword Salute. If the Senior Officer feels that the report is so short that the Junior Officer should stand at salute while making the report, he does not acknowledge the salute until the termination of the conversation, whereupon the Junior Officer will stand at salute until it is acknowledged by the Senior Officer and come to a carry simultaneously with the Senior Officer. If, however, the Senior Officer acknowledges the salute immediately and resumes at carry, the Junior Officer should resume carry with him and again salute at the termination of the conversation. After the Commandery has been declared open, all salutes must be by sword.)

(In the formation of these Ceremonies or Tactics for the Asylum, space and size of the usual Asylum has been given much consideration, and therefore, the number of Sir Knights employed is based on free movements, but should space permit, larger numbers should be used.)

a. The Tactical Unit should consist of the Officers and at least twelve Sir Knights.

b. In the event of more than twelve Sir Knights being used, all comply with the movements as herein specified.

(It is the duty of the Captain General to see that all preparations are made for the Conclave of the Commandery. If work is contemplated, all the necessary paraphernalia should be in readiness. The Captain General should attend to this, but may delegate one or more of the Junior Officers or Sir Knights to assist in making preparations.)

(The Commandery should always be opened promptly at the time fixed by the By-Laws and always in full form, if possible, except at Inspections, when the full form is to be exemplified in the work later on. The hour having arrived the Captain General reports to the Commander, wherever he may be in the Asylum, but not in his station. All salutes will be by hand until the Commandery is formed and the order to draw swords is given. Junior Officers will salute by hand unless the Senior or Commanding Officer has his sword drawn. (See Ritual, page 91, Lines 1 and 2.) (Captain General takes his station.)

C. G.:— Sir Knight Warder (hand salute) Sound the assembly. Officers take your stations. Sir Knights be seated.

(The W. when directed to sound the assembly, may do so by the use of a bugle, or he may go to the door and invite the Sir Knights to enter the Asylum; closes the door and takes his station (hand salute) and is seated. The stations of the absent officers should now be filled by the C. G., who will then direct the S. W., to ascertain if all present are Knights Templar.)

C. G.:—Sir Knight Senior Warden: (S. W., arises, faces C. G., hand salutes.) Are all present Knights Templar?

S. W.:—Sir Knight Junior Warden: (J. W., arises and hand salutes.) Ascertain if all on the North are Knights Templar.

(If necessary, S. W., examines those on the S., J. W., those on the N. Then they will meet in the West and the J. W., will report to S. W.; then both proceed to their stations and the S. W., will salute C. G., and report, J. W., stands at his station facing C. G., until after report, both are then seated.)

S. W.:—Sir Knight Captain General, all present are Knights Templar.

(During the foregoing inspection if any person is unknown to a Warden, he faces the individual and says: Are you a Knight Templar? (If negative answer), PLEASE RETIRE. (If positive answer), Can any Sir Knight vouch for you?

(If a Knight competent to do so, can vouch for the visitor as a Knight Templar in good standing and is sitting near him, the Warden may accept the voucher and pass on. Otherwise the Warden causes the visitor to arise, faces the East salutes, and when the salute is acknowledged, reports:)

S. W.:—Sir Knight Captain General, I find a visitor whom I do not know to be a Knight Templar.

C. G.:—Can any Sir Knight present vouch for the visitor?

(Upon which any Knight present, competent to do so, may arise, salute the C. G., with hand, and when the salute is acknowledged, say:)

Sir Knight Captain General, I vouch for this visitor as a Knight Templar.

C. G.:—Sir Knight Senior (or Junior) Warden, a Sir Knight has vouched for the visitor.

(If no Knight vouches for the visitor, the C. G., will say:)

C. G.:—The visitor will retire to the ante-room, where an examining committee will wait upon him.

(The visitor does so. The Warder will open the door, see that the visitor retires and returns to his seat. The Warden faces and pursues his examination. The Examining Committee should be appointed and retire immediately after the Wardens are seated.)

C. G.:—Sir Knight Warder (hand salute). Post the Sentinel, inform him that a Commandery of Knights Templar is about to be opened and direct him to guard accordingly. (See Ritual.)

W.:—(hand salute) Sir Knight Captain General, the Sentinel is at his post and the Asylum is duly guarded.

FULL FORM OPENING

Reception

C. G.:—Sir Knight Senior Warden: (S. W., arises, facing C. G., hand salutes.) 1. Form the Lines for the Reception of the Commander.

(S. W. takes position on the right of the proposed line and faces West, draws sword and commands:)

S. W.:—1. Commandery, 2. ATTENTION. (All arise). (At the command "fall in," all not excused, without drawing swords, promptly fall in, single rank, facing to the right, graduated in size from front to rear. The J. W. falls in on left of rank.)

C. G.:—All Sir Knights not in line be seated.

(C. G., now takes his station in front of the center of the Commandery. S. W., now takes position facing Commandery and two paces in front of the center.)

S. W.:—1. Left, 2. FACE, 3. Draw, 4. SWORDS.

(For instruction and with inexperienced commands, the S. W., may, if necessary, dress the Commandery to the right before presenting it to the C. G., although the dress is not part of the authorized formation.)

S. W.:—1. Count, 2. TWOS.

(The S. W., should then designate the left of the First Platoon and the right of the Second Platoon.)

S. W.:—1. Present, 2. SWORDS.

(S. W., faces about, salutes the C. G., who has taken position in front of the Commandery, and reports.)

S. W.:—Sir Knight Captain General, the lines are formed.

(The C. G., returns salute, draws sword, and commands.)

C. G.:— 1. Carry, 2. SWORDS.

(The S. W., without command, faces right and takes his post as right guide, by shortest route.)

C. G.:—1. Open ranks, 2. MARCH, 3. FRONT.

(At the first command, The S. W., and J. W., step backward six steps and mark the new alignment of the rear rank. The C. G., goes to the right flank and sees that the guides are in line parallel to the front rank, then places himself, facing the left three paces in front of the right file and commands:)

C. G.:—1. MARCH.

(The front rank, the odd numbered Knights dress to the right without closing interval; the even numbered Knights who constitute the rear rank, cast their eyes to the right, step backward, halt a little in rear of the alignment, then dress to the right without closing intervals, on the line established by the guides. The C. G., superintends the alignment of the front, and rear ranks, then places himself, facing the left, three paces in front of the right file, and gives the command.)

C. G.:—1. FRONT.

(The guides resume their places in the front rank, the Knights of both ranks cast their eyes to the front.)

C. G.:—1. Form two divisions, 2. Files, 3. COVER, 4. Front Rank, about, 5. FACE.

(At the command "cover," the rear rank files take two right steps (10 inch step) and become the first division. At the command "face," the front rank faces about and becomes the second division. The right guide (S. W.) will execute about face, march forward one pace beyond the line of the first division, halt, right face and march in rear of first division and take post on left of first division opposite Junior Warden. The C. G., now takes his station in the East.)

C. G.:—Sir Knight Junior Warden, (J. W. steps to the center of the lines, faces East and salutes) with the Standard Guard as escort, repair to the apartment of the Commander and inform him the lines are formed for his reception. (J. W., after receiving the orders from the C. G., salutes, faces about, steps forward, and commands.)

(When J. W., approaches the Escort, the Warder will quickly pass in rear of Standard Guard and take his place on south side of Asylum Door and Salute Escort as it passes out, remaining at door until Escort and Grand Officer and his staff, if he has one, has entered, when he will return to his station.)

J. W.:—Standard Guard as escort, 1. Right, 2. FACE, 3. Forward, 4. MARCH, 5. Column right, 6. MARCH.

(Escort proceeds to the apartment of the Commander through the Asylum door. On arriving in Commander's apartment, the J. W., at right of escort, commands:)

J. W.:—1. Escort, 2. HALT, 3. Right (or left), 4. FACE, 5. Present, 6. SWORDS; (and saluting says:)

J. W.:—Eminent Commander, the lines are formed for your reception, and the escort awaits your pleasure.

(No banners are carried by Standard Guard.)

Commander:—It is my pleasure to be escorted into the Asylum.

J. W.:—1. Carry, 2. SWORDS, 3. Right (or left), 4. FACE, 5. Forward, 6. MARCH.

(The C. G. and P., follow the escort in single file, swords at sides, except Commander, who has his sword hooked up. As escort enters the Asylum through Asylum door, the Warder will salute and announce:)

W.:—The Eminent Commander Approaches.

(After Escort passes, W., will take station.)

C. G.:—1. Sir Knights, 2. ATTENTION.

(All knights not in line will rise, but not draw swords.)

C. G.:—Present, 2. SWORDS.

(All not in line will uncover, and so remain until the command "carry, swords," when they will recover. The escort will be marched to the front of their stations in the West, when the J. W., will command:)

J. W.:—1. Escort, 2. HALT, 3. Right, 4. FACE, 5. Present, 6. SWORDS, takes his post opposite the S. W., and comes to Present.

(The C., followed by the G. and P., after leaving the escort, pass through the lines to the East, each taking his station. The C., and he only, uncovers when passing through the lines. When near the East, he will be saluted by the C. G. On arriving at his station he will about face, draw sword, and command:)

Commander:—1. Carry, 2. SWORDS. All Sir Knights not in line, be seated.

FULL FORM OPENING
Rehearsal

Commander:—For rehearsal: 1. Officers, 2. POST.

(The G., and C. G., will leave the dais together, the G., sword drawn, taking his position on the left of the second division and the C. G., on the right of the first division. The

C., takes position two paces to the right and midway between and facing the lines and proceeds as follows:)

TO COMMUNICATE ACROSS THE LINES.

C: Fst. Div:—Com. to the Scd. Div., the P. W. W. 1. GUARD, 2. GIVE CUTS or PARRY FOUR. (W. given) 3. Carry, 4. SWORDS.

(At command "carry" come to the position of Guard. At command "swords" come to the position of "carry swords.")

C: Scd. Div.:—Com. to the Fst. Div. the P. P. W. 1. GUARD, 2. GIVE CUTS or PARRY FOUR. (W. Given) 3. Carry, 4. SWORDS.

(At command "carry" come to the position of Guard. At command "swords" come to the position of "carry swords.")

C: 1. Return, 2. SWORDS. (Commander will also return sword.)

C: Fst. Div.:—Com. to the Scd. Div., the I. W. 1. S. Ks., 2. KNL. (Place right foot forward one pace, kneel on left knee) 3. Un., 4 CV., 5. Dep., 6. CHPH., 7. Intrlc., 8. FNGS., 9. COMMUNICATE. (W given)

C:—1. Sir Knights, 2. Secure, 3. CHAPEAUX, 4. Re., 5. COVER, 6. ARISE.

(Commander, Generalissimo and Captain General will now take their stations in the East.)

FULL FORM OPENING
Inspection

Commander:—Sir Knight Captain General, (hand salute) 1. Form the lines for Inspection and Review (C. G., draws sword and commands:)

C. G.:—For Inspection and Review, 1. Officers, 2. POST.

(and takes his station in front of Commandery. S. W., takes post on right of First Division, C. and G., take stations in front of Commandery in rear of Captain General.)

C. G.:—1. Reform Line, 2. Second Division, about, 3. FACE, 4. Close ranks, 5. MARCH.

(At command "face," the Second Division executes "about face" and at the command "march," the rear rank marches by left oblique to their places in line.)

C. G.:—1. Right, 2. DRESS, 3. FRONT.

C. G.:—1. Draw, 2. SWORDS, 3. Second Platoon, left step, 4. MARCH, 5. HALT. Commandery, 1. Present, 2. SWORDS. Standard Guard, 1. POST.

Sw. B.:—Standard Guard, 1. Carry, 2. SWORDS, 3. Forward, 4. MARCH.

(Upon reaching the interval prepared for the Standard Guard will command:)

Sw. B.:—Standard Guard, 1. Right wheel, 2. MARCH.

(Passing through interval, then left about, and then left oblique into line.)

Sw. B.:—1. Right, 2. DRESS, 3. FRONT, 4. Present, 5. SWORDS.

C. G.:—Commandery, 1. Carry, 2. SWORDS. Prepare for Inspection 1. Open ranks, 2. MARCH, 3. FRONT.

(At first command, the S. W. and J. W,, step backward, six backward steps, to mark new alignment of rear rank. The C. G., goes to the right flank and sees that guides are on a line parallel to the front rank, then takes position facing the left, three paces in front of right file and commands:)

C. G.:—1. MARCH.

(At command "march," the Standard Guard takes two paces forward; the odd numbered Knights dress to the right without closing interval; the even numbered Knights cast their eyes to the right, step backward, halt a little in rear of alignment, and then dress to the right without closing intervals on the line established by the guides. The C. G., superintends the alignment of front rank and verifies the alignment of rear rank, then places himself facing the left, three paces in front of the right file and gives the command:)

C. G.:—1. FRONT.

(and takes his position in front of the center of the Commandery. At the command "front," S. W. and J, W,, take positions two paces in front of the center of their respective platoons, on line with Standard Guard, C. G., faces the Commander, who has taken his position in front of the Commandery, sword salutes and reports:)

C. G.:—Eminent Commander, the lines are formed.

(The Commander accompanied by the G. (Commander has his sword hooked up on first ring) will then inspect the lines, passing first in front of the C. G., then in his rear to the right of the lines; the C. G. facing about. commands:)

C. G.:—1. INSPECTION SWORDS.

(and again faces to the front. The Knights successively execute Inspection Swords. S. W. and J. W., stand at "carry swords," when being inspected. After inspecting lines, the Commander will take position in front of the center of the Commandery, G., takes position one pace to rear and two paces to right of C.)

FULL FORM OPENING
Review

C.:—Sir Knight Captain General, 1. PASS IN REVIEW.

(C. G., salutes, faces about, and commands:)

C. G.:—1. Close ranks, 2. MARCH.

(At command "close ranks" the Wardens face Right and Left, Standard Guard will about face. At the command "march" they march to their places in line. The C. G., may dress the line if he desires.)

C. G.:—1. Count, 2. THREES 3. Pass in Review, Right by Threes, 4. MARCH.

(When column arrives near the North side of Asylum C. G., commands:)

C. G.:—1. Form Platoons, 2. Column Left.

S. W.:—1st Platoon, 1. Threes Left.

J. W.:—2nd Platoon, 1. Continue the march.

C. G.:—3. MARCH.

(At the command "march," first platoon executes threes left, S. W., takes position two paces in front of center of his platoon commands:)

S. W.:—1. GUIDE RIGHT.

(The second Platoon continues in column of Threes until in proper position, then J. W., Commands:)

J. W.:—1. Second Platoon, 2. Threes left, 3. MARCH, 4. GUIDE RIGHT.

(J. W., should be two paces in front of center of second Platoon. C. G., takes post three paces in front of the S. W. When six paces from reviewing officer, C. G., commands:)

C. G.:—1. Eyes, 2. RIGHT.

(and at same time executing Salute Swords. After passing six paces beyond the Reviewing Officer, C. G., will Command:)

C. G.:—1. FRONT.

(When the first Platoon is six paces from the Reviewing Officer, S. W. commands:)

S. W.:—1. Eyes, 2. RIGHT.

(at the same time executing sword salute. After passing six paces beyond Reviewing Officer, S. W., will command:)

S. W.:—1. FRONT.

(Second Platoon, will also execute above movements at proper time at command of Junior Warden. Beauceant is dipped.)

C. G.:—1. Column of threes, First Platoon, right by threes, (S. W. cautions, right by threes) 2. MARCH.

(After Second Platoon has passed reviewing officer six paces, the J. W., commands:)

J. W.:—1. **Front,** 2. **Second Platoon, right by threes,** 3. **MARCH.**

(The column is then marched to the place of formation.)

C. G.:—1. **Threes left,** 2. **MARCH,** 3. **Commandery,** 4. **HALT.**

(He dresses the line if necessary.)

C. G.:—1. **Present,** 2. **SWORDS.**

(The C. G., from the center of the lines faces about and salutes the Commander, who responds with hand salute. If the Commander wishes to exercise the Commandery in the Manual of the Sword, or otherwise, he commands.)

C.:—**Sir Knight Captain General, 1. To your post.**

(C. G., will return sword and take post on the left of the Commander one pace in rear. The Commander will draw sword and command:)

C.:—1. **Carry,** 2. **SWORDS.**

(and may exercise the Knights in the Sword Manual or other Drills, closing with "carry, swords.") (Commander returns sword.)

FULL FORM OPENING
Triangle
(Should be formed near center of Asylum)

C.:—**Sir Knight Captain General: Form the Triangle preparaory to our Devotions.**

(C. G., will salute with hand, take his position in front of the center of the Commandery, draw sword, face the lines and command:)

C. G.:—1. **Present,** 2. **SWORDS,** 3. **Standard Guard,** 4. **POST.**

Sw. B.:—1. **Standard Guard,** 2. **Carry,** 3. **SWORDS,** 4. **Forward,** 5. **MARCH,** 6. **Left Wheel,** 7. **MARCH:** (on arriving at station) 8. **Left About,** 9. **MARCH,** 10. **Standard Guard,** 11. **HALT.**

C. G.:—1. **Carry,** 2. **SWORDS,** 3. **First Platoon, Left Step,** 4. **MARCH:** (closing interval) 5. **HALT.**

Commandery:—1. **Return,** 2. **SWORDS,** 3. **Threes Right,** 4. **Close Order,** 5. **MARCH.**

(The threes will wheel to the right; the first three will halt on the completion of its wheel; the remaining threes will continue the march until within facing distance.)

C. G.:—1. **Left,** 2. **FACE.**

(The divisions will face to the left, the third being in front, the first in the rear. C. G., then goes directly to his station in the East and commands:)

C. G.:—1. To Form Triangle, 2. Officers, 3. POST, 4. MARCH.

(The S. W., will about face, pass by the right and rear of the column and take position on the left of the First Division; the J. W., on the left of the Third Division each facing their division. The Standard Bearer, Sword Bearer and Warder will march from the West in close order to within four paces of the Divisions, when the Warder will move by left oblique, a distance from the Standard Bearer equal to the length of the Division, halt and face to the front, and the Sword Bearer will move by right oblique to the left of the Second Division, halt and face his division. The Standard Bearer will march forward one pace beyond the head of the lines, halt and about face.)

C. G.:—1. FORM TRIANGLE.

S. W.:—1. First Division, 2. Stand Fast. (He then faces to the left.)

Sw. B.:—1. Second Division, 2. Left Wheel. (He then faces to the left and acts as a moving pivot for the Second Division.)

J. W.:—1. Third Division, 2. Forward, 3. Guide Left. (He then faces to the left.)

C. G.:—1. MARCH.

(The Third Division will move forward until opposite the Warder, when the J. W., will command:)

J. W.:—1. Third Division, 2. HALT, 3. About, 4. FACE.

(The Standard Bearer will march forward as soon as the Second Division has wheeled past him, to within one pace of the Second Division, halt, and about face with the Second Division; the Second Division having wheeled 90 degrees.)

Sw. B.:—1. Second Division, 2. HALT, 3. About, 4. FACE, 5. Right, 6. DRESS, 7. FRONT.

S. W.:—1. First Division, 2. Left, 3. DRESS, 4. FRONT.

J. W.:—1. Third Division, 2. Right, 3. DRESS, 4. FRONT.

(After the Divisions have been aligned, the Captain General will command:)

C. G.:—1. First and Third Divisions, 2. Inward Wheel, 3. MARCH, 4. Divisions, 5. HALT.

(C. G., then returns sword and reports; hand salute.)

C. G.:—Eminent Commander, the Triangle is formed.

C.:—Sir Knights on sidelines, 1. ATTENTION.

C.:—Sir Knights Generalissimo, Captain General and Excellent Prelate, 1. ACCOMPANY ME TO THE TRIANGLE.

(All Officers on dais descend and halt at foot of dais to give Prelate an opportunity to enter the Triangle. G. and C. G., will precede the C., by one step in completing the Triangle. After command "accompany me to the Triangle," the Commander, Generalissimo and Captain General will immediately Secure Swords before leaving their stations and enter the Triangle (drop swords). On arriving at the Triangle, the Commander will command:)

C.:—1. Sir Knights, 2. To your devotions, 3. KNEEL, (Com., also kneels), 4. Un-COVER.

(The Sir Knights at the Triangle will execute all commands and all other Sir Knights will uncover and recover only upon command of the Commander. After devotions, the Commander will recover, arise and command.)

C.:—1 Sir Knights, 2. Re-COVER, 3. ARISE.

(The C., G., C. G. and P,, then return to their stations as follows: They about face, secure swords, march forward in a direct line to the foot of the dais, opposite their stations, halt permitting the Prelate to take his station and then the other three officers ascend dais, about face, drop swords and remain standing.)

C.:—1. Sir Knight Captain General, (hand salute) 1. REDUCE THE TRIANGLE.

C. G.:—(sword drawn) commands: 1. Form Square, 2. First and Third Divisions, 3. Backward Wheel, 4. MARCH, 5. Divisions, 6. HALT.

(When divisions have formed in a hollow square, Captain General commands:)

C. G.:—1. Officers, 2. TO THE CENTER AND FRONT.

(The Sw. B. and S. W., will take position on the right of the St. B., the War., and J. W., on the left,)

C. G.:—1. MARCH.

(They will then march to the front, guide on the St. B. halt, completing the square, and give hand salute, which will be acknowledged by all officers on the dais.)

C. G.:—1. Form two divisions, 2. Second Division Right and Left Backward Wheel, 3. MARCH, (when on line with others) 4, HALT.

(The Second Division divides in the center, and the right half thereof wheels backward to the left, and the left half thereof wheels backward to the right thus forming two parallel lines or two divisions, facing each other. The then First Division, which is facing to the North, should dress to the right, and the then Second Division, which is facing South should dress to the left, both divisions dressing without command.)

C. G.:—1. Officers, 2. About, 3. FACE, 4. Commandery, 5. Draw, 6. SWORDS, 7. Present, 8. SWORDS, 9. Officers, 10. POSTS.

S. W.:—1. Officers, 2. Carry, 3. SWORDS, 4. Forward, 5. MARCH.

(The officers will pass through the lines, the S. W. and J. W., dropping off the line at their stations if lines permit, if not, go to end of lines and right and left to their stations, the Standard Guard continuing to their stations. The Sword Bearer then commands:)

Sw. B.:—1. Standard Guard, 2. HALT, 3. About, 4. FACE.

(When the above has been executed, the Captain General will then command:)

C. G.:—1. Carry, 2. SWORDS, 3. Return, 4. SWORDS, 5. About, 6. FACE, 7. BE SEATED.

(The Captain General will then face the Commander and report:)

C. G.:—1. Eminent Commander your order has been obeyed.

FULL FORM OPENING
Rehearsal of Duties.

(When the Commander first addresses the Generalissimo, the latter will answer with hand salute and at close of the conversation will again salute with hand, and when acknowledged by the Commander, will be seated until called upon the second time, when he will draw his sword and make proper sword salute. As the Commander addresses the other officers, except the Prelate, who salutes by bowing, such officers will execute Sword Salute and if acknowledged by the Commander, come to Carry Swords, and remain so until end of conversation, when they will again execute Sword Salute, and when acknowledged by the Commander, resume Carry Swords and stand at attention until close of Rehearsal. The Prelate stands at attention after reciting his part; or the E. C., may before the R. D., begins, direct the C. G., to call all officers to ATTENTION and to DRAW SWORDS; the R. D., then proceeds. The following commands will be used in executing the above change when used:)

C.:—Sir Knight Captain General, you will call all officers to ATTENTION and to DRAW SWORDS.

(Captain General will hand salute when Commander calls on him and at close of order of the Commander will draw his sword before communicating the order to the officers.

The Generalissimo will also execute the commands of the Captain General.)

C. G.:—1. Officers, 2. ATTENTION, 3. Draw, 4. SWORDS.

(giving the above commands, the C. G., will not salute the Commander, but will stand at attention at "carry swords." The Commander will then begin R. D.)

(After the order of the Commander has been communicated through the Generalissimo, (Ritual 97-35) the Captain General faces the Commandery and commands:)

C. G.:—1 Sir Knights, 2. ATTENTION, 3. Draw, 4. SWORDS, (Ritual 98-4).

(C. G., then communicates the order and commands)

C. G.:—1. Present, 2. SWORDS.

(C. G., then reports to Generalissimo, who reports to Commander (Ritual 98-9.) Commander rises, draws sword and states:)

C.:—I now declare_____Commandery No. _____, opened in due form, 1. Sir Knights, 2. Carry, 3. SWORDS. Sir Knight Warder, Inform the Sentinel, etc. (Ritual 98-12).

W.:—(Opens door and says) Sir Knight Sentinel, etc. (Ritual 98-13-14 and rubric following.)

W.:—Eminent Commander: Your order, etc. (Ritual 98-15.)

C.:—1. Sir Knights, 2. Return, 3. SWORDS, 4. Be Seated.

(During the opening ceremonies none should be admitted; but at this point the Warder may report the alarms which he has heard, and, on direction from the Commander, admit the Sir Knights who may be waiting.)

INSPECTION OF CONSTITUENT COMMANDERY BY GRAND COMMANDER OR HIS REPRESENTATIVE

(While an inspection by the Grand Commander or his Representative differs only in a few instances from a combination of a Full Form Opening and Reception of Distinguished Guests, so many questions arise as to proper titles and movements, it is thought advisable to set out the main features under separate titles.)

(The Commandery should be opened in SHORT FORM. The Grand Commander, if making the Inspection, or his Representative making the Inspecton, should notify the Grand Warder, or if he is not present, appoint an Acting Grand Warder, who for that Inspection becomes Grand Warder by title, to report to the Sentinel that he desires to enter and for what purpose. The Sentinel then gives the proper battery and waits until it is answered from the inside by the Warder of the Commandery; Sentinel then opens door and announces:)

S.:—The Grand Warder for the Grand Commander. (If it is the Deputy Grand Commander, he would announce:)

S.:—The Grand Warder for the Deputy Grand Commander. (If for any other Grand Commandery Officer, he would make the same announcement, except changing the official title to conform to the official title of the officer he is announcing. If it is a Past Grand Commander, he would announce:)

S.:—The Grand Warder for a Past Grand Commander. (If it is a Past Commander, he would announce:)

S.:—The Grand Warder for a Past Commander.
(THE USE OF PERSONAL NAME OF GRAND WARDER OR ANY OTHER OFFICER EXCEPT WHEN THEY ARE ACTUALLY BEING INTRODUCED, IS NOT DESIRABLE.)

(Immediately upon hearing the alarm, the Warder of the Commandery will arise, draw sword, salute the Commander, and report:)

W.:—Eminent Commander, there is an alarm.

Commander:—Sir Knight Warder, ascertain the cause of the alarm.
(Commander returns salute, thus releasing the Warder, who then goes to the door, gives battery, and after it is answered and door opened by the Sentinel and his report made, Warder returns to his station, salutes the Commander and reports:)

W.:—Eminent Commander, the alarm was caused by the Grand Warder for the Grand Commander, (or giving the official title of the officer represented.)

C.:—Permit him to enter.
(Commander then acknowledges salute, thus releasing the Warder, who then goes to the door, gives battery and when door is opened by Sentinel, states:)

W.:—The Commander permits him to enter.
(Warder salutes the Grand Warder with salute swords as he enters, comes to Carry Swords after he has passed, remains at door until the Grand Warder retires, again saluting him as he goes out, then comes to Carry Swords and returns to his station.)

(After permission is given the Grand Warder to enter, he comes in, goes up South side of Asylum, to about one-half the distance to the East, turns left to center of Asylum, faces East and reports:)

G. W.:—**Eminent Commander, I am directed to report that the Grand Commander, (or using official title of party making the Inspection) is in waiting to inspect your Commandery.**

C.—**Eminent Grand Warder, inform the Grand Commander, (or if other officer using proper official title) that an escort will immediately wait upon him.**

(The Grand Warder salutes, executes carry swords, retires reversing inward movement and reports to the Grand Commander, (or Inspecting Officer) as follows:)

G. W.—**Right Eminent Grand Commander, (or if other officer, use proper official title) the Commander of_____ Commandery No._____ directs me to inform you that an escort will immediately wait upon you.**

(THE LINES ARE THEN FORMED IN ACCORDANCE WITH THE FULL FORM OF THIS GRAND JURISDICTION. AFTER THE LINES ARE FORMED, THE JUNIOR WARDEN IS IN THE WEST, AT THE LEFT OF THE SECOND DIVISION. THE CAPTAIN GENERAL THEN COMMANDS:)

C. G.—**Sir Knight Junior Warden, (The J. W. steps to the center of the lines, faces the East and salutes:) Be in readiness to march the Standard Guard as escort to the apartment of (giving proper official title of Inspecting Officer.) The J. W., faces about, steps forward and commands:)**

J. W.:—**Standard Guard as Escort, 1. Right, 2. FACE.**

(The Captain General reports.)

C. G.:—**Eminent Commander, the lines are formed and the escort is in readiness.**

C.:—**Sir Knight Generalissimo, with the Standard Guard as escort, you will repair to the apartment of the Grand Commander (or official title of Inspecting Officer) and inform him that the lines are formed for his reception.**

(The G., salutes with hand, repairs to the escort and directs the J. W., to proceed, and takes his post in rear of Escort.)

J. W.:—**1. Escort, 2. Forward, 3. MARCH.**

(When G., approaches the J. W., the Warder will quickly pass in rear of Standard Guard and take his place on south side of Asylum door and salute escort as it passes out, remaining at door until escort and Grand Officer and his staff, if he has one, has entered, when he will return to his station. He will also stand at salute when the above escort, Grand Officer and staff enter. The J. W., conducts the Escort to the apartment of the Grand Commander, (or other officer) and on arriving at the apartment the J. W., at the right of Escort commands:)

J. W.:—1. Escort, 2. HALT, 3. Left (or Right), 4. FACE, 5. Present, 6. SWORDS.

(J. W., saluting. The Inspecting Officer, with those accompanying him on his left, should be standing opposite the escort. The G., steps forward, salutes with hand, and says:)

Generalissimo:—**Right Eminent Grand Commander**, (or proper title if other officer) I have the honor to inform you that the lines are formed for your reception. The Escort awaits your pleasure.

Grand Commander, (or Inspecting Officer) Sir Knight Generalissimo, it is my pleasure to be escorted into the Asylum.

(G., salutes and same is acknowledged by Inspecting Officer or Grand Officer, after which the G., steps to left of Inspecting Officer or Grand Officer and takes him by left arm to escort him into Asylum.)

(IT MUST BE DEFINITELY UNDERSTOOD THAT THE GENERALISSIMO, WHO HAS BEEN SENT OUT BY THE COMMANDER, IS THE ONLY ONE THAT CAN PERSONALLY ESCORT THE GRAND COMMANDER OR HIS REPRESENTATIVE INTO THE ASLYUM. IF THE COMMANDER HAS DESIGNATED SOME OTHER SIR KNIGHT TO FORM THOSE OF THE STAFF WHO ARE IN THE APARTMENT. IT DOES NOT GIVE THEM ANY AUTHORITY TO PERSONALLY ESCORT THE RANKING OFFICER WHO IS BEING RECEIVED.)

J. W.:—1. Escort, 2. Carry, 3. SWORDS, 4. Left (or Right), 5. FACE, 6. Forward, 7. MARCH.

(After giving the command "face," J. W. will take station on opposite end of line and Standard Guard will return to Asylum in reverse order. As the Escort, with the Grand Commander, (or Inspecting Officer) approaches the Asylum door, the Warder will announce:)

W.:—The R. E., Grand Commander (or if other officer, using proper title) approaches.

(The Escort will be marched to the front of their stations in the West, when the Junior Warden will command:)

J. W.:—1. Escort, 2. HALT, 3. Right, 4. FACE, 5. Present, 6. SWORDS.

(J. W., then takes his post opposite the Senior Warden. The Standard Bearer and Sword Bearer will remain at Present Swords until released by commanding officer. NO BANNERS WILL BE CARRIED OUT OF THE ASYLUM WHEN GOING OUT AS ESCORT IN RECEIVING THE GRAND COMMANDER OR INSPECTING OFFICER.)

(As soon as the Warder announces the Grand Commander or Inspecting Officer, the Captain General will command:)

C. G.:—1. Commandery, 2. ATTENTION.

(As the Grand Commander or Inspecting Officer reaches the foot of the lines, the Captain General will command:)

C. G.:—1. Form Arch of Steel, 2. Cross, 3. SWORDS.

(After above commands have been executed, the Generalissimo and Grand Commander (or Inspecting Officer) pass through the lines to the East, he only uncovering when Generalissimo says:)

(C. G., should order carry swords as soon as Gen., and Grand Commander (or Inspecting Officer) has passed through the Lines.)

G.:—Eminent Commander, I have the honor to present Sir Knight_____ (using full name), Right Eminent Grand Commander.

(If another Officer is making the Inspection, his name and title should be given. For example as follows:)

G.:—Eminent Commander, I have the honor to present Sir Knight_____, Eminent Grand Senior Warden, representing the Grand Commander.

C.:—Right Eminent Grand Commander, it gives me pleasure to welcome you to our Asylum. I now surrender to you my chair of office and ask you to preside over this Conclave.

(If the Inspection is made by the Deputy Grand Commander, he will be addressed as Very Eminent Deputy Grand Commander. If by any other Grand Commandery Officer, as Eminent (using proper title.) If by a Past Grand Commander, as Right Eminent Past Grand Commander. If by a Past Commander, as Eminent Past Commander.)

(The Grand Commander or Inspecting Officer may take charge of the Commandery, or make brief response. returning the Command to the Commander. If the Grand Commander or Inspecting Officer has a staff and wishes to introduce them, he should do so at this time while in command, and if he desires to do so, the entire staff having stopped at the foot of lines, each member passes through separately, halts, recovers and salutes the Presiding Officer, being presented and accorded the proper honors due their station or rank. They will step up on the dais and be introduced, and after being introduced will face the Commandery, saluting with hand and after being invited to take a seat either on the dais or the side lines, will again salute the Presiding Officer, then take seat. If any of the staff are to be introduced, all in the staff must be presented and introduced.)

(The GRAND MASTER OF THE GRAND ENCAMP-MENT, HIS REPRESENTATIVES; PAST GRAND MASTERS; The GRAND COMMANDER, HIS REPRESENTATIVES; AND PAST GRAND COMMANDERS ARE THE ONLY ONES EN-TITLED TO BE RECEIVED UNDER AN ARCH OF STEEL. (Grand Encampment Regulation) OTHER GRAND OFFI-CERS, PAST COMMANDERS AND PRESENT COMMANDERS ARE RECEIVED AT "PRESENT SWORDS." ALL SHOULD WEAR SWORDS WHILE BEING RECEIVED THROUGH THE LINES, AND THEY SHOULD HAVE THEM HOOKED UP ON THE FIRST RING.)

(The Generalissimo immediately goes to his station after the Commander has welcomed the Grand Commander or In-specting officer.)

(If the Grand Commander or Inspecting Officer has a staff and does not wish to take command, the staff, who have been held at the foot of the lines, will pass separately through the lines with the honors due their rank, received by the Com-mander by a hand clasp welcome and directed to a seat. Af-ter all have been received and seated, the Commander will di-rect the Captain General to dismiss the lines as follows:)

C.:—Sir Knight Captain General, Dismiss the lines.

C. G.:—1. Return, 2. SWORDS, 3. BE SEATED.
(NUMEROUS INTRODUCTIONS BECOME OBNOXIOUS TO THOSE ON THE SIDE LINES AND SHOULD BE AVOID-ED.)

(The Full Form Opening is then followed and just before the lines are formed for inspection, the Commander, accom-panied by the Inspecting Officer and Generalissimo, takes posi-tion in the North, which temporarily becomes the East and must be so considered with reference to commands and move-ments. The Commander takes position in the center and in front of and facing the Commandery. The Inspecting Officer takes position on his right facing the Commandery. The Generalissimo takes position 2 paces in rear and one pace to the right of the Inspecting Officer. After the lines are form-ed, the Capt. General reports to the Commander as follows:)

C. G.:—"Eminent Commander, the Lines are formed."

E. C.:— (reports to the Inspecting Officer using the proper title) "The Lines are formed for your in-spection."

(The Inspecting Officer may then invite the Commander or the Commander and Generalissimo to accompany him on his inspection, both having swords hooked up and the Commander on his right. The Inspecting Officer then inspects the lines passing first in front of the Capt. General then in his rear to the right of the lines; the Capt. General facing about commands:)

C. G.:—"Inspection Swords."

and again faces to the front. The Knights successively execute "Inspection Swords." None of the officers execute "Inspection Swords," but remain at "Carry Swords" while being inspected. After inspecting the rear of the last line, the Commander and Inspecting Officer pass around the right flank to their positions in the North. The Inspecting Officer should at this time direct the Commander to have the Commandery pass in review.

Commander: (does not draw sword) Sir Knight Capt. General, Pass in Review.

(The Full Form Opening is then continued. After the Review, the Commander may execise the Commandery in the Manual of the Sword, after which the Commander, Inspecting Officer, and Generalissimo leave their temporary stations in the North and return to their regular stations in the East where they remain until the completion of all work and the Commandery closed. The Inspecting Officer should always be the first to be called on for remarks, after the Full Form Opening and Rehearsal of Duties, and he should not leave the asylum until the Commandery is closed.

ALTERNATIVE FORMING OF TRIANGLE PERMISSABLE

To form Triangle from Line in South position after Review, Standard Guard in line. The C. G., divides the Commandery into three equal Divisions, and has them count off, according to the number of Knights in each division:

C. G.:—To Form Triangle, Officers, POSTS.

(The S. W. steps two paces to front, faces left; the J. W., steps two paces front, faces right (if there are more than three in each Division), the Sw. B. and W., step two paces front, face Sw. B., right, W. left, simultaneously all march; the S. W., to the left of first Divsion, J. W. to right of third Division, Sw. B., to right; W. to left of second Division; face the line, take position on respective Flanks. The Knights on those flanks step back one pace, face to right and left, and take positions made vacant by the officers.)

C. G.:—Form Triangle, First Division, STAND FAST, Second and Third Divisions, Forward, Right Wheel, MARCH.

(The second division arriving at a right angle to first division.)

Sw. B.:—Second Division, HALT, Right, DRESS, FRONT.

J. W.:—Third Division, Right Wheel, MARCH.

(The third division continues the wheel, on J. W., as pivot, until at a right angle with second division, when,)

J. W.:—Third Division, HALT, Right, DRESS, FRONT.

C. G.:—First and Third Divisions, Inward wheel, MARCH, HALT.

(The C. G., returns to his station, salutes, and reports:)

C. G.:—Eminent Commander, The Triangle is Formed (Returns sword).

(The Commander rises.)

C.:—Sir Knights, Generalissimo, Captain General and Prelate, accompany me to the Triangle. (See Ritual. Done Together.)

C.:—On Left Knee, KNEEL, Uncover.

(At command kneel, all step back 24 inches with left foot, and kneel.)

C.:—RECOVER, ARISE, Sir Knight Captain General, REDUCE THE TRIANGLE.

(The C. G., and P., return to stations.)

C. G.:—Form Square, First and Third Divisions, Backward Wheel, MARCH, HALT, Sir Knights, Draw, SWORDS, Second and Third Divisions, About, FACE, Form Line.

S. W.:—First Division, Stand Fast.

Sw. B.:—Second Division, Forward, Left Wheel.

J. W.:—Third Division, Forward, Left Wheel.

C. G.:—MARCH.

(When the second division is in line with first division, Sw. B., commands:)

Sw. B.:—Second Division, Forward, MARCH.

(Passing the line of first division two paces,)

Sw. B.:—Second Division, HALT, About, FACE.

(Taking his position on left of first division,)

Sw. B.:—Second Division, Right, DRESS, FRONT.

(When the third division has completed wheel of ninety degrees,)

J. W.:—Forward, MARCH.

(When flank of second division cleared:)

J. W.:—Left Wheel, MARCH, Forward, MARCH.

(Passing line of second division two paces.)

J. W.:—HALT, About, Face.

(Taking his position on left of second division,)

J. W.:—Right, DRESS, FRONT.

C. G.:—Officers, POSTS.

(The S. W., J. W., Sw. B, and W, and Sir Knights, return to posts in line in reverse order to that in preparing to form Triangle.)

C. G.:—Commandery, ATTENTION, Draw, SWORDS, Present, SWORDS, Colors, POST.

Sw. B.:—Standard Guard, Carry, SWORDS, Forward, Guide Center, MARCH.

(When St. G. passes center of Asylum two paces:)

Sw. B.:—Standard Guard, Left Wheel, MARCH, Forward, MARCH.

(Arriving at West:)

Sw. B.:—Standard Guard, Left About, MARCH, HALT, Present, SWORDS.

C.:—Sir Knights, Senior and Junior Wardens: To Your Stations.

(The Wardens step two paces to front, S. W. faces left, J. W. faces right, march to center, halt, both face left, proceed to stations. Come to Salute swords.)

C.:—Commandery, Carry, SWORDS, Return, SWORDS, BE SEATED.

SUPPLEMENTAL TACTICS

Prepared by George F. Dix, R. E. P. G. C. For use when more than 64 Sir Knights are in line for the opening of a Commandery of Knights Templar in Full Form. Adopted in 1928.

RECEPTION of COMMANDER

C.—S. K. C. G., see that the Asylum is in suitable array for my reception.

S. K. G., and E. P., accompany me to my apartment.

C. G. (sword drawn)—S. K. Warder, sound the assembly. (done).

Officers take your stations. S. Ks., be seated.

S. K. S. W., are all present Knights Templar? (ritual.)

S. W.—S. K. C. G., all present are Knights Templar. (seated).

C. G.—S. K. Warder, post the Sentinel; inform him that a Commandery of Knights Templar is about to be opened and direct him to guard accordingly.

W.—S. K. C. G., the Sentinel is at his post and the Asylum is duly guarded.

C. G.—S. K. S. W., form the lines for the reception of the C.

S. W.—Commandery—Attention. Fall In. Right, Dress. Front. (all S. Ks., not in line be seated).

Draw, Swords.

Count 4s. Count 8s. Right Face. 8s Left front into line, March. Halt. Left, Face.

S. K. C. G., the lines are formed.

C. G.—Officers, Posts.

(The S. W. takes post on the right of the fourth division and the J. W. takes post on the left of the fifth division).

Form Divisions.

S. W.—First, Second, Third and Fourth Divisions, Stand Fast.

J. W.—Fifth, Sixth, Seventh and Eighth Divisions, Forward, Guide Left, March. Halt. About, Face. Right, Dress. Front. (Do not close intervals in dressing. The fourth and fifth divisions should be five feet apart, and in center of the Asylum.)

C. G. (in the East)—S. K. J. W. (The J. W. steps to the center of the lines, faces the East and salutes). Repair with the St. G. as escort, to the apartment of the C., inform him that the lines are formed, and await his pleasure. The J. W., faces about, steps forward and commands:

St. G. as Escort—Right, Face. Forward, March, and conducts it to the apartment of the C. (through door in northwest corner of Asylum, if possible), the W. stopping inside the door. On arriving, the J. W. at right of escort commands:

Escort, Halt. Right (or Left), Face. Present, Swords, and saluting, says:

J. W.—E. C.—The lines are formed for your reception, and the escort awaits your pleasure.

C.—It is my pleasure to be escorted into the Asylum.

J. W.—Carry, Swords. Right (or Left), Face. Forward, March. The C., G., and P. follow the escort in single file, swords at side. As the escort enters the Asylum the W., saluting, announces: The E. Commander approaches. Warder then takes his station. All Knights not in line will rise, but do not draw swords.

C. G.—Present, Swords. (All not in line, will uncover, and so remain until the command Carry, Swords, when they will recover). The escort will be marched to the front of their stations in the West, when the J. W. will command: **Escort, Halt, Left, Face. Present, Swords,** and passing in rear of the eighth division, takes his post at the left of fifth division opposite the S. W., and comes to present. If the St. B., carries the Beauseant he will salute with it, at the command **Present Swords.** The C., followed by the G. and P., after leaving the escort, passes through the lines to the East, each taking his station. The C., and he only, uncovers when passing through the lines. When near the East he will be saluted by the C. G. On arriving at his station he will about face, draw sword, and command: **Carry, Swords.** All Knights not in line; be seated.

REHEARSAL.

E. C.—S. K. C. G., Form the lines for Rehearsal._

C. G.—For Rehearsal—Officers, Posts. Form Divisions.

S. W.—First, Second, Third and Fourth Divisions, About, Face.

Fourth Division, Stand fast·

First, Second and Third Divisions, take distance. March. Halt.

First and Third Divisions, about, Face. Dress to the east, Front.

J. W.—Fifth, Sixth, Seventh and Eighth Divisions, About, Face.

Fifth Division, Stand fast.

Sixth, Seventh and Eighth Divisions, Take distance. March. Halt.

Sixth and Eighth Divisions, About, Face. Dress to the east. Front.

(The G. takes post at the head of the Sixth division; the C. G., at the head of the third division, both facing west; the S. W., at the foot of the third division and the J. W., at the foot of the sixth division, each facing east; each Warden passing in rear of his division.)

The C., will step down to the head of the lines, then:

C. G.—E. C.—The lines are formed.

(Ritual.) The words need not be passed through the St. G.

INSPECTION AND REVIEW.

If Inspection and Review are to follow Rehearsal then:

C.—S. K. C. G.—Form the lines for Inspection and Review.

C. G.—For Inspection and Review—Officers, Posts.

The S. W. takes position on the right of the first division.

The J. W., takes position on the right of the eighth division.

The C. and G. resume their stations.

C. G.—Draw, Swords. Close, Divisions.

S. W.—First and Third Divisions—About, Face.
J. W.—Fifth and Seventh Divisions—About, Face
C. G.—Close, on First Division. March. Halt.

Divisions, Left, Face. Right by 4s. Guide Left
March, (around hall) Commandery, Halt. Left, Face
Commandery, Present, Swords. Colors, Post.

The Sw. B. will then command: St. G.—Carry
Swords. Forward, Guide center, March.

The St. G. will then March straight to the front to
a little beyond the right of the Commandery, when the
Sw. B. will command: St. G.—Halt; at this point the
C. and G. rise and salute. The C. G. salutes the Color
as they pass.

Sw. B.—About, Face. Forward, Guide Center
March. And upon reaching the interval prepared for
the Colors, will give the command: St. G.—Left Wheel
March, and upon the arrival at one pace in the rear o
their place in the line: St. G.—Halt. About, Face
Right, Dress. Front. Present, Swords.

C. G.—Commandery—Carry Swords. Right
Dress. Front. Prepare for Inspection. Open Ranks
March.

At the Command Open Ranks, the Wardens take
six steps to the rear. At the Command March, the St
G. steps three paces to the front.

(No. 4 stands fast. No. 3 steps back two paces
No. 2 steps back four paces. No. 1 steps back six
paces.)

S. W.—Commandery—Right, Dress.

C. G.—Front.

At the command Front, the Wardens march three
paces to the front of the front rank, and take post on
a line with the St. G., the S. W. opposite the center o
the right platoon, and the J. W. opposite the center o
the left. The C. G. takes post in front of the St. G.
faces the C. and reports:

C. G.—E. C.—The lines are formed. He then face
to the front. The C., accompanied by the G. and dis
tinguished visiting Knights whom he may invite, who
follow in single file, swords at side, will then inspec
the lines, passing first in front of the C. G., who sa
lutes, then in his rear to the lines, when the C. G., fac
ing about, commands: Inspection. Swords, and again

faces the front. The officers and Knights sucessively execute the three motions of inspection swords, commencing when the C., or Inspecting Officer, approaches within two paces, and coming to carry swords when he has passed. The C., and those with him, will now pass in front of the S. W., St. G. and J. W., thence by their rear to the right of the front rank, and along its front; thence by its rear to the right of the second rank, and along its front, thence by its rear to the right of the third rank and along its front, and thence by its rear to the right of the fourth rank and along its front, thence by its rear to the right, and to his position for review, which is in the North, opposite the center of the lines. The G., takes post on the right and one pace in the rear of the C. Distinguished visitors accompanying the Commander on his tour of inspection should at this point be on the left of the Commander. During the tour of inspection the distinguished visitors should follow the Commander and in front of the G. The Grand Commander, his Representative, the Inspecting Officer or ranking officer should station himself on the right of the Commander and in front of G., when at Review.

(Here the sword drill may be given if desired, in which case C., will say: S. K. C. G.—To your post. C. G. salutes, returns sword, and takes position on left of C., one pace to the rear.)

C.—S. K. C. G.—Pass in Review.

C. G.—Close Ranks, March. At the command Close Ranks, the Wardens right and left face, the St. G., about faces; at Command March, the Wardens and St. G., march to their places in line and face to the front, the rear ranks close up.

S. W.—Commandery—Right Dress, Front.

C. G.—Commandery—Right, Face. Pass in Review. Forward, Guide Left, March.

Column Left, March. Guide Right. Column Left, March. Eyes Right. Front. Guide Left. Column Left, March. 4s Left, March. Halt. Right Dress. Front. Present, Swords.

C.—S. K. C. G.—Form the Triangle preparatory to our devotions. (returns his sword, and with the G., and staff repair to their stations and be seated.)

TO FORM TRIANGLE AFTER REVIEW

C. G.—Colors, Post.

Sw. B.—St. G.—Carry Swords. Forward, Guide Center, March. Right Wheel, March, and when a little beyond the right of the Commandery; St. G.—Halt. About, Face; or, To the Rear March. Forward, Guide Center, March. St. G.—Halt. About, Face.

C. G.—Commandery—Carry, Swords. Return, Swords.

First Platoon—Left Step, March. Halt. (to close interval)

Commandery—Right Dress, Front. Count 6s. 6s Right, Close Order, March.

Commandery—Left Face. (No. 1 and No. 2 S. Ks. constituting First Division; No. 3 and No. 4 S. Ks., constituting Second Division; No. 5 and No. 6 S. Ks., constituting Third Division.)

C. G.—Officers, Posts.

The S. W. takes post on the left of the first division, which is in rear, and the J. W., on the left of the third division, which is in front, the second division being in the middle. The Sw. B., St. B. and W., march from the West to the base of the triangle; then the Sw. B., moves by the right flank to the left of the second division, halts and faces to the left, and the W., moves by the left flank a distance from the St. B., equal to one-half the length of the division, halts and faces to the right, when the following commands are given:

C. G.—Form Triangle.

S. W.—First Division—Stand Fast.

Sw. B.—Second Division—Left, Face. Forward, Column Right.

J. W.—Third Division—Forward, Guide Left.

C. G.—March.

The third division moves forward opposite the W., then:

J. W.—Third Division—Halt. About, Face. After first and second divisions have dressed, then comes: Right, Dress. Front. The second division files past the Sw. B., who stands fast, and as its left closes on the W., the Sw. B., commands: Second Division—Halt. Right Face. After first division has dressed its line then: Right, Dress. Front.

S. W.—First Division—Left Dress, Front.

. The St. B., takes three steps forward as soon as the third division passes him. If carrying banner he stands at order, and uncovers and recovers at the proper time; if not, he kneels, etc., at the commands.

C. G.—First and Third Divisions—Inward Wheel, March. Halt.

C. G.—E. C.—The Triangle is formed. (Ritual.) The Triangle May be Reduced Thus:

(The C. G. and P., having taken their stations.)

C.—S. K. C. G.—Reduce the Triangle. The command will be given:

C. G.—Officers—To the Center, March.

The S. W., J. W., Sw. B., and W., will immediately march to the front, about three paces in front of the base of the Triangle, with the St. B., in the center thereof, the Sw. B., on his right and the S. W., on the right of the Sw. B.; the W., on the left of the St. B., and the J. W., on the left of the W. All of these officers will dress to the center.

C. G.—Form Lines. Right and Left Backward Wheel, March. The first division wheels backward to the right; the second division divides in the center, and the right half thereof wheels backward to the left, and the left half thereof wheels backward to the right; the third division wheels backward to the left, thus forming two parallel lines facing each other. Halt. The then first division, which is facing to the north, should dress to the right, and the then second division, which is facing south, should dress to the left, both divisions dressing without command. When the lines are thus formed.

C. G.—Divisions, Halt. Draw, Swords. Officers, About; Divisions, Right and Left, Face. (All face west, the officers advancing to the foot of the lines.)

C. G.—Forward, March. (C. G. marches with the lines.) When the line of officers reaches the station of Standard Guards: C. G.—Halt. Officers, About; Divisions, Inward, Face. Present, Swords. C. G. faces C.. salutes and reports.

C. G.—E. C.—Your order has been obeyed.

C.—Commandery—Carry, Swords. Officers, Posts. Return, Swords. Be seated.

RECEPTION of
DISTINGUISHED GUESTS

(The following form of reception should only be used at Grand Commandery Conclaves when it is desired to be slightly more formal, and when there are quite a number of distinguished guests present from other jurisdictions. While the question probably will never arise, if it should, officers of equal rank from different grand jurisdictions should take rank according to the dates of their charters from the Grand Encampment. At Annual Conclaves, the Representatives of the Grand Master is always the ranking officer, even if the Grand Master is present. If this form is used, the Grand Commander should appoint some past officer, preferably a Past Grand Commander to retire and arrange the distinguished guests according to their rank and a "Personal Escort," should be appointed for each Distinguished Guest, other than the Ranking Guest. IT IS ALWAYS THE DUTY AND RIGHT OF THE GRAND GENERALISSIMO TO ESCORT THE RANKING GUEST AND TO INTRODUCE HIM IN THE ASYLUM. The Personal Escorts retire to the Reception Room and are formed in line and await the arrival of the Grand Generalissimo and Regular Escort, as shown in the title, "Inspection of Commandery by the Grand Commander or His Representative." The lines are formed in the Asylum in accordance with the Full Form Opening, the Past Officer having formed his line and counted off in twos, will instruct the Grand Captain of the Guard to give the proper battery and when answered by the Grand Warder, will report to the Grand Warder that "Distinguished Guests desire admission." The Grand Warder will report to the Grand Commander as follows:)

G. W.:—Right Eminent, Grand Commander, Distinguished Guests desire admission.

G. C.:—Eminent Grand Warder, direct the Grand Captain of the Guard to instruct the Distinguished Guests that an Escort will immediately wait upon them.

G. C.:—Eminent Grand Generalissimo, with the Standard Guard, as Escort, repair to the Reception Room and tender the Escort to the Distinguished Guests to conduct them into the Asylum.

(Escort marches out as shown under the title, "Inspection of Commandery by the Grand Commander or His Representative." On arrival in the Reception Room, and when properly aligned, the Grand Generalissimo will address the Distinguished Guest as follows:)

G. G.:—Distinguished Guests, the Grand Commander tenders you an Escort into the Asylum.

(The ranking Distinguished Guest will accept the Escort

72

In such language as he may desire to use. If there is but one Guest, he will be addressed by his proper title. The Escort will then return to the Asylum with the Distinguished Guests in column of twos, the Escort returning to its post; the Grand Warder having announced as the Escort approached as follows:)

G. W.:—The Escort with Distinguished Guests.

(Immediately upon the announcement of the Grand Warder the Grand Captain General will command:)

G. C. G.:—1. Grand Commandery, 2. ATTENTION, 3. Sir Knights not in line, 4. UNCOVER.

(All on side lines arise and uncover, remaining uncovered until the last distinguished Guest has been received and the Grand Captain General commands, Be Seated. The Distinguished Guests, with the Grand Generalissimo and the ranking Guest at the head, stop at the foot of the lines, when the Grand Captain General will command:)

G. C. G.:—1. Sir Knights, 2. Form Arch of Steel, 3. Cross, 4. SWORDS.

(Or "Present Swords" if the rank of the Distinguished Guest does not entitle him to be received under an Arch of Steel, the proper honor should be accorded. The Grand Generalissimo, with the ranking Guest, will then pass through the lines, the Guest being on the right of the Grand Generalissimo, the Guest only uncovering as they pass through. As soon as each Distinguished Guest has passed through the lines, the Grand Captain General will command:)

G. C. G.:—1. Carry, 2. SWORDS.

(The Grand Generalissimo will then present the Distinguished Guest as follows:)

G. G.:—Right Eminent Grand Commander, I have the honor of presenting, (for example) "Sir Knight, John Doe, Right Eminent Grand Commander of the Grand Commandery of Illinois."

(When the Guest reaches the head of the lines he recovers and after above presentation, salutes the Grand Commander, who takes him by the hand and assist him to the dais and welcomes him, introducing him to the Grand Commandery, as follows:)

G. C.:—Sir Knights, I have the pleasure and honor of introducing to you, (for example), "Sir Knight, John Doe, Right Eminent Grand Commander of the Grand Commandery of Illinois." After which the Guest will face the Grand Commandery, salute and then face the Grand Commander, who will invite him to be seated. On receiving the above invitation to be seated the

73

Guest will salute the Grand Commander and take the seat offered. All salutes will be by hand. Each Guest should then pass through the lines the same as outlined above and be presented by the personal Escort assigned him and introduced by the Grand Commander. The same procedure should be followed until all Guests have been introduced. The Guest should not be invited to make any remarks at this time. If the Guest is entitled to preside, the Grand Commander should tender him his chair of office as set out in the Reception of the Grand Commander. When all have been received, the Grand Commander will command:

G. C.:—Sir Knight Grand Captain General, 1. DISMISS THE LINES.

(The Grand Captain General will then command:)

G. C. G.:—1. Sir Knights, 2. Return, 3. SWORDS, 4. BE SEATED.

CEREMONY for RECEPTION of the UNITED STATES FLAG

The Grand Encampment at Miami approved and recommended the reception of the United States Flag into the Asylum, and we would recommend that same be done with the following ceremony:

Before the opening the United States Flag will be placed in the reception room and the Commander should appoint a Guard of Honor consisting of four Sir Knights, one of whom will be the commanding officer in the ceremonies. Past Commanders may be used if desired. Before any work whatever is started, all officers will take their stations upon a signal or order of the Commander and will vacate them at the conclusion of the Flag ceremony upon a signal or order of the Commander. The Guard of Honor may be formed either in front of the Captain General's station or in the West, at or in front of the Standard Guard. If in the latter place, some of the following commands will not be needed, but we will show the formation in the East.

C.:—**Guard of Honor,** you will retire and present the United States Flag.
(The Captain of the Guard will take position in line with and six paces from Captain General's station and command:)

C. G.:—1. **Guard of Honor,** 2. **FALL IN,** 3. **Left, 4. FACE,** 5. **Draw,** 6. **SWORDS,** 7. **Forward,** 8. **MARCH.**
(When about on line with preparation room door, the C., of the G., will command:)

C. G.:—1. **By the Left Flank,** 2. **MARCH.**
(On arriving in the West, the C. of the G., will command:)

C. G.:—1. **Column left,** 2. **MARCH.**
(After crossing the Asylum in front of the Standard Guard, the C. of the G., will command:)

C. G.:—1. **Column right,** 2. **MARCH.**
(As the Honor Guard reaches the West, the Warder will go to Asylum door and open same and remain there until after the Honor Guard has returned to the Asylum, making his announcement of the approach of the Guard from that point. The Honor Guard passes out into the reception room, about faces, the center Sir Knight taking the flag and returns to the Asylum without any alarm. The return is in a column of files as they went out except the Sir Knights are reversed. As soon as the Guard passes out the Commander will command:)

C.:—1. Commandery, 2. ATTENTION, 3. Draw, 4. SWORDS.

(When the Guard approaches on return, the Warder will announce:)

W.:—**Eminent Commander,** the United States Flag with its Guard of Honor.

(The Commander will immediately command:)

C.:—1. Commandery, 2. Present, 3. SWORDS.

(On arriving in Asylum where movement can be made, the C. of the G., will command:)

C. G.:—1. Column left, 2. MARCH.

(When Flag is in front of the Standard Guard, the C. of the G. will command:)

C. G.:—1. By the Right Flank, 2. MARCH.

(The Guard of Honor will march up center of Asylum and when four paces of the dais, the Captain of the Guard will command:)

C. G.:—1. HALT. (Those on the dais will salute the flag with hand.)

(The C. of the G., will then salute the Commander with officers present and when answered by the Commander with hand salute, will come to carry and proceed as follows:)

C. G.:—**Eminent Commander,** By authority of the Grand Encampment of the United States of America, we present to you the United States Flag. Its place is on the dais at your right. As Knights Templar we pledge ourselves to protect and defend this emblem of our Country, and to yield up our lives rather than forfeit our pledge.

C.:—**Sir Knight,** Justly we honor this Flag, symbol of the Government that protects our precious heritage. A heritage preserved by the noble sacrifices and true devotion of a united people. A heritage which under the gracious favor of our Heavenly Father we fervently pray may be transmitted in full measure to our posterity. Its colors, like those of our Grand Standard, remind us of purity and honor, justice and sacrifice, the finest fruits of Christian civilization.

C.:—**Captain of the Guard, CAUSE THE FLAG TO BE PLACED IN ITS STATION AT MY RIGHT.**

C. G.:—**1. Honor Guard, 2. Present, 3. SWORDS, 4. Sir Knight Flag Bearer, 5. PLACE THE UNITED STATES FLAG.** (C. of the G., then comes to officers present.)

(The Flag Bearer will go in direct line and place Flag in proper station, hand salute the Flag, about face and return to his place in line from the rear. The Commander then commands:)

C.:—1. Carry, 2. SWORDS. (Entire Commandery comes to Carry. The C. of the G., then commands:)

C. G.:—1. Guard of Honor, 2. About, 3. FACE, 4. Forward, 5. MARCH.

(And when in the West in front of Standard Guard will command:)

C.G.:—1. Guard of Honor, 2. HALT, 3. About, 4. FACE.

(The Commander then commands:)

C.:—1. Commandery, 2. RETURN, 3. SWORDS, 4. BE SEATED.

RED CROSS FULL FORM OPENING

(The lines are formed and the S. M., received according to the Tactics of the jurisdiction unless otherwise provided by the Ritual or Regulations of the Grand Encampment.) (Following page 5 of Ritual.)

P. M. P.—Comp. M. C.—Form the lines for the reception of the S. M.

(M. C., takes position on the right of the proposed line and faces West, draws sword and commands:)

M. C.—1. Companions, 2. ATTENTION. (All arise) 3. FALL IN.

(At the command "fall in," all not excused, without drawing swords, promptly fall in, single rank facing to the right, graduated in size from front to rear. The M. I., falls in on left of rank.)

P. M. P.—All Companions not in line be seated.

(P. M. P., now takes his station in front of the center of the Council. M. C., now takes position facing the line and two paces in front of the center.)

M. C.—1. Left, 2. FACE, 3. Draw, 4. SWORDS, 5. Count, 6. TWOS, 7. Present, 8. SWORDS.

(M. C., faces about, salutes the P. M. P., who has taken position in front of the Council, and reports:)

M. C.—P. M. P., the lines are formed.

(The P. M. P. returns salute, draws sword, and commands:)

P. M. P.—1. Carry, 2. SWORDS.

(The M. C. without command, faces right and takes his post as right guide, by shortest route.)

P. M. P.—1. Open ranks, 2. MARCH, 3. FRONT.

(At the first command, the M. C. and M. I., step backward six steps and mark the new alignment of the rear rank.

The P. M. P., goes to the right flank and sees that the guides are in line parallel to the front rank, then places himself, facing the left, two paces in front of the right file, and commands:)

P. M. P.—MARCH.

(The front rank, the odd numbered Companions dress to the right without closing interval; the even numbered Companions who constitute the rear rank, cast their eyes to the right, step backward, halt a little in rear of the alignment, then dress to the right without closing intervals, on the line established by the guides. The P. M. P., superintends the alignment of the front and rear ranks, then places himself, facing the left, two paces in front of the right file, and gives the command:)

P. M. P.—FRONT.

(The guides resume their places in the front rank, the Companions of both ranks cast their eyes to the front:)

P. M. P.—1. Form two divisions, 2. Files, 3. COVER, 4. Front Rank, 5. About, 6. FACE.

(At the command "cover," the rear rank files take two right steps (10 inch steps) and become the first division. At the command "face," the front rank faces about and becomes the second division. The right guide (M. C.) will execute about face, march forward one pace beyond the line of the first division, halt, right face and march in rear of first division and take position on left of first division, opposite M. I. The P. M. P., now takes his station in the East.)

P. M. P.—Comp. M. I., (M. I. steps to the center of the lines, faces East and salutes.) With the Standard Guard as escort, repair to the apartment of the S. M., and inform him the lines are formed for his reception.

(M. I., after receiving orders from the P. M. P., salutes faces about, steps forward, and commands:)

M. I.—1. Standard Guard as escort, 2. Right, 3. Face, 4. Forward, 5. MARCH, 6. Column right, 7. MARCH.

(When M. I., approaches the Escort, the Warder will quickly pass in rear of Standard Guard and take his place on south side of Audience Chamber Door and salute escort as it passes out, remaining at door until Escort and S. M., has entered, when he will return to his station. On arriving in S. M's., apartment, the M. I., at right of escort, commands:)

M. I.—1. Escort, 2. HALT, 3. Right (or left), 4. FACE, 5. Present, 6. SWORDS.

(M. I. salutes S. M., and reports.)

M. I.—Sovereign Master, the lines are formed for your reception, and escort awaits your pleasure. (No banners are carried by Standard Guard.)

S. M.—It is my pleasure to be escorted into the Audience Chamber.

M. I.—1. Carry, 2. SWORDS, 3. Right (or left,), 4. FACE, 5. Forward, 6. MARCH.

(The S. M., P. C, and E, H, P,, follow the escort in single file swords at sides except S. M. who has his sword hooked up. As escort enters the Audience Chamber through Chamber door the Warder will salute and announce:)

W.:—The Sovereign Master. **P. M. P.**—1. Present, 2. SWORDS.

(After escort passes, Warder will take station. All Companions not in line will rise, but not draw swords, if equipped with swords, but will uncover and so remain until the command "**carry, swords,**" when they will recover. The escort will be marched to the front of their stations in the West, when the M. I., will command:)

M. I.—1. Escort, 2. HALT, 3. Right, 4. FACE, 5. Present, 6. SWORDS.

(The M. I., then takes his post opposite the M. C., and comes to Present. The S. M., followed by the P. C. and E. H. P., after leaving the escort, pass through the lines to the East, each taking his station. The S. M., and he only uncovers when passing through the lines. When near the East, he will be saluted by the P. M. P. The S. M, on arriving at his station, will about face, draw sword, and command:)

S. M.—1. Carry, 2. SWORDS. Let the words be communicated.

(The Ritual will then be followed as shown, commencing at the top of page 6, followed by the Rehearsal of Duties as set out in the Ritual.)

CONFERRING the ILLUSTRIOUS ORDER of the RED CROSS.

The Red Cross Opening starting at page 5 of the Ritual should be observed whenever the Order is conferred, with possibly the following exception. At an Annual Inspection, if the Order of the Red Cross is to be conferred, if time does not permit, the Order may be opened in short form, following as near as possible the short forms of opening as shown on page 131 of the Ritual, changing the titles and nomenclature where necessary. Asylum Tactics for full form opening in the Order of Red Cross, reception of the Sovereign Master, or of Distinguished Guests are included in this Manual and are supplemental to the Red Cross opening as set out in the Ritual.

In conferring the Order of the Red Cross, the Asylum becomes the Audience Chamber and the titles change as follows:

> The Commander becomes Sovereign Master
> The Generalissimo becomes Prince Chancellor,
> The Captain General becomes Prince Master of the Palace,
> The Senior Warden becomes Master of Cavalry,
> The Junior Warden becomes Master of Infantry, (also Companion Conductor.)
> The Prelate becomes Excellent High Priest,
> The Treasurer becomes Master of Finance,
> The Recorder becomes Master of Despatches

All other officers retain the same title as in the Order of the Temple.

After the Reception of the Sovereign Master and Distinguished Guests, if there are any, the Words will be communicated either as set out in the Ritual, or according to the Tactics of the Jurisdiction. We would recommend the latter to obtain uniformity in all the Orders, and they are herewith set out for your guidance:

S. M.:—1. Carry, 2. SWORDS. Let the Words be communicated. The P. M. P. then takes command.

P. M. P.—1. First Division communicate to the Second Division the J. P., 2. GUARD, 3. GIVE CUTS or PARRY FOUR, 4. COMMUNICATE, (W. given), 5. Carry, 6. SWORDS.

P. M. P.—1. Second Division communicate to the First Division the P. C., 2. GUARD, 3. GIVE CUTS or PARRY FOUR, 4. COMMUNICATE, (W. given), 5. Carry, 6. SWORDS.

P. M. P.—1. First Division communicate to the Second Division the R. C. W., 2. GUARD, 3. GIVE CUTS or PARRY FOUR, 4. COMMUNICATE, (W. given), 5. Carry, 6. SWORDS.

P. M. P.—1. Second Division communicate to the First Division the Sign, Grip and Word of a Companion

)f the Illustrious Order of the Red Cross, 2. GUARD,
3. COMMUNICATE, (S., G. & W. given), 4. Carry, 5.
SWORDS.

After devotions and the return of swords as ordered by the Sovereign Master, the signs will be given and
ines dismissed, then followed by the Rehearsal of
Duties as defined in the Ritual, starting at page 7.

The Work.

The actual conferring of the Order will then be
started as shown on page 11 of the Ritual. There are
three principal parts to the work: namely, The Grand
Council, The Journey and The Audience Chamber. Size
and number of rooms may make some variations necessary in some commanderies. All necessary preparations should be made in advance and every effort made
to avoid delays between the different parts.

The Grand Council

We believe it advisable to confer all the work in
the Audience Chamber, rather than use two rooms,
thus avoiding the necessity of those on the side lines
changing from one room to another in order to view
the work.

The E. H. P., Warder and those who are to be in
the Grand Council (not less than six councilors and
two attendants for the E. H. P.) should retire and put
on appropriate robes, either in a side room or in the
Sentinel's Room, if no other available. The M. I. should
have the candidate in the preparation room, and cloth-
ed as a R. A. M.

The Warder takes charge of the Grand Council,
and being on the right and in front of the Grand Council, marches them into the Audience Chamber in order.
If there is a stage, dais or platform, the E. H. P., and
one attendant on each side should sit on the stage,
dais or platform, and the other members of the Grand
Council should be stationed on the floor in front of the
E. H. P., formed in two rows, the lines being slightly
farther apart at the front than at the rear, and far
enough apart at the rear so that the M. I., and the
candidate can sit across at the rear of the lines and not
be behind any of the members of the Council. When
marching the Grand Council into the Audience Chamber, they should enter at the Sentinel's door, column

left, then right and pass in front of their chairs, the inward face by command of the Warder; the Hig Priest with his two attendants in the rear will pas through the lines and take their places at their sta tions. All will be seated when instructed to do so b the E. H. P.

When the M. I. brings in the candidate, the should come in from the preparation room, advance u the North side of the Audience Chamber, column righ and stand in front of the chairs that have been place for them at the foot of the lines. They will not b seated until the E. H. P., directs them to do so.

The C. C., will gird. Z. (cand.). The W., will hav scabbard ready. The first attendant will produce th sword, and the second attendant the sash and han them to the E. H. P., for presentation.

The Grand Council will retire in order with the E H. P., leading through the lines, followed by the at tendants and councilors, who will countermarch in ward, right and left, following the column in twos, ou of the room through the Sentinel's door. Warde should march at the front and Sentinel opens doo both in the opening and closing of the Grand Counci

The Journey.

If there is a stage or platform large enough, th third guard should be on the stage or platform. I not, the bridge should be in the East, placed crosswis of the room; the Jewish Banner on the North side o end of the bridge and the Persian Banner on the Soutl side or end of the bridge.

The two Jewish Guards should be stationed, on just inside of the Audience Chamber, near the pre paration room door and the other about three-fourth the distance to the North end of the bridge.

A guard tent may be set up in the room. If sc plug in a lamp cord in the floor socket and cover a re globe with red tissue paper and a few sticks to repre sent a camp-fire. Turn off all other lights except a din light. Two guards recline at the fire. First P., guar is on duty near the South end of the bridge; Z., passe bridge and when he attempts to proceed, the challeng is given. The second and third P., guards do not dra swords, but rush forward, when called, one to each side and sieze Z., by the arms, the first P., guard holding him at the point of the sword. When Z., is disarmed, one guard at a time retains hold, one procuring the garb and the other the fetters. THE ACTION SHOULD BE SNAPPY AND REALISTIC.

If more than one candidate, each must pass over the bridge separately, the work to be exemplified on the first and last candidate, all to be introduced into tne Audience Chamber immediately following the first candidate. If any of the candidates are not challenged, they should be placed so that they can see the work exemplified on the last candidate to pass the bridge.

On entering the Audience Chamber, the M. of C., is in command and at the front or head of the column. Next should be the C. C., then the last candidate to pass the bridge, Z., garbed and fettered, followed by the other candidates, each accompanied by a guard on his right, and when they swing and face the East, the guards will be behind their candidates, the C. C., on the right of the principal candidate. The C. C., speaks for the candidates and all candidates arise and are seated upon each occasion, with the C. C.

The Audience Chamber.

The Court of D., should be as brilliant and regal as circumstances will permit, using as many robed princes and rulers as the circumstances will permit. If there is a stage, dais or platform, it should be used, or at least a raised platform for the S. M. All members of the court should be in proper position before the curtain is raised, or if the court is placed on the floor, it is suggested that a curtain be placed across the Chamber, and this drawn back after the court is properly placed. Guards, torch bearers, slaves, etc., may be used where there is a historical basis in the Ritual for their use, but nothing shall be done that detracts from the solemnity and dignity of the Order, or serves to detract the minds of the candidates from the beauty and purpose of the lessons sought to be conveyed. The S. M., should be in the center in the East, with the P. C., on his right and the P. M. P., on his left, the latter two slightly more to the front than the S. M· The

Princes and Rulers should be in triangular lines, the apex toward the S. M. The M. of F., should be the last man on the North line toward the Chamber and the M. of D., at the same end of the opposite line. Chairs for the C. C., and the candidates should be placed across the Audience Chamber, at a distance from the East that will permit of them getting the most clear view of the court scene. The Warder during all the ceremonies of this Order has his station in the West and quite near the preparation room door. On addressing the S. M., the Princes and Rulers should arise and bow slightly in suitable salutation. The work should be done with dignity and decorum. When the M· of C., enters the room with the candidates, will march directly up the North side of the room to about the center, then column right until directly in front of the S. M., in the center of the room, thus having the M. of C., C. C., and candidates in the front line, with the guards directly behind the candidate that they are guarding. There should be two attendant guards other than those with the candidates, they to carry the sword and sash, marching in the rear, and after the others have lined themselves, these guards will march around the ends and between the Princes and Rulers and carry the sword and sash to the front for the use of the S. M. These guards will then take position at the ends of the second line and when the S. M. commands, "Strike Off," will advance and remove garb and fetters from the candidate and give them to the Warder, who should be on hand to receive them. Guards then take their former stations.

When called upon to invest Z., the P. M. P., will arise, bow, and pass inside lines and stand in front of Z. Robe and crown will be brought up by the Warder, who will place robe on Z. P. M. P., will tie cord or fasten clasp at the front, and receiving crown from the Warder, places it carefully on the head of Z., using both hands in doing so. He then places his right hand, palm down, arm extended over the head of Z., and exclaims as per Ritual. The entire line, with P. M. P. at front, M. of C., next, then C. C., candidates and guards on the right of candidates will face the South, march, column right twice, cross the Chamber, column right again and march up the North side of Chamber until near the East, then column right again, the C. C., and candidates going in front of chairs that have been placed for them across the room, the P. M. P., turning left to his station, the M. of C., turning right, after P. M. P., has turned left, and goes to his station, the guards turning right and passing down the South side of room and taking position in the West.

It is advisable to have an ancient altar, and when the S. M., directs the M. of F., to bring forth the altar, he will retire with the guards to the Treasury and bring forth the Ancient Altar and place it in front of the S. M. Bible with S. and C., properly displayed should be on the altar. The guards take positions in the West after placing the altar.

Music may be used to relieve the abruptness of changes of scenes. The M. of D., will present the S. M., with scroll and quill. He also reads the decree when ordered to do so by the S. M. The S. M., will arise and pronounce the promulgation sentence (the last line) with wave of scepter.

When the banner of the Order is called for, the guards stationed in the West will take it from its station in the West, march up the South side of the Chamber, to the East and the guard carrying the banner will hold it so that it can be plainly seen by the candidates and so hold it until after the explanation, when the banner will be placed on the left of the Sovereign Master, in the East, and guards will then resume their stations.

The Historical Lecture should always be given either by the S. M., or a competent companion. This lecture attempts to remind the candidate of the lessons he has been given in the conferring of the Order.

ORDER of MALTA

There is such a complete explanation of the costumes, settings and movements for this Order set out in the Ritual that very little explanation is necessary. The Order is without doubt, the most religious of any of the Orders conferred in York Rite Masonry. No commands should be given in a loud or boisterous manner, but all should be solemn, dignified and imposing. The music should be "Cathedral" in character. The dais is in the East. Immediately in front of it is a table with a red cover on which should be painted—or embroidered—in white, the upper and transverse limbs of a Latin Cross, according to the design as shown on page 38 of the Ritual. The table in the West should be covered with red, having painted on it a large black octagon block figure, on which should be painted a white Maltese Cross (eight points), the points extending to the outer angles of the octagon figure, according to the design as shown on page 38 of the Ritual.

The five Ceremonial Banners should be placed on the South side of the Chapel, if possible, beginning in the West with the White Banner, then the Red, Black, Purple and Yellow. (If the room is not large enough to place all in the South, they may be divided with some on the North.) During the ceremony each Banner should have a guard.

The officers, guards of the banners, and the eight Knights who are to be seated at the Table in the West, all properly costumed, will assemble in a room adjoining the Chapel, and form in procession as per Ritual.

The procession enters the Chapel to appropriate music. (ALL SWORDS IN SCABBARDS.) The front of the column halts in the East and the whole line fronts, the C. G., remaining at the head of the line. When the line has come to front, the Chaplain, with Bible on a black cushion, followed immediately by the Prior with the Lieutenant Commander on his left, will pass in front of line until they reach the East, when they will column left, march across the East and around the north end of table and take their stations. The line with C. G., leading will march around the Chapel to their stations. The Grand Banners first drop out, the one dropping out first to take one pace and remain in that position until the other Grand Banner is directly opposite him, then both take stations simultaneously. As the line passes behind the Table in the West, the leading Table in the West Knight starts circling around the table followed by the others who are to be at the table. The C. G., C. of O., and M., halt in the West until the five ceremonial Banner Guards close the interval, when the C. of O., columns right, the five Guards following him out of the Chapel; he then returns and takes his station; the C. G., and M., column left and march to their stations. When the C. of O. is ordered to post guards, he goes out, brings them in, and places them at their stations. They will then place Banners in the proper receptacles. The C. of O., faces about when all are stationed and marches to his station in the West.

In the recessional, the C. G., leads off the C. of O., having gone to the front and falling in behind the C. G., followed by the Grand Banners, Marshal, the eight at table in the West Knights, five Banner Guards, the White Banner Guard falling in first and followed by the others in order of their stations. Then they form line on North side of Chapel and face front, allowing the Chaplain, Prior, with Lieutenant Commander on his left, to pass out of the Chapel. No salutes will be given on the recessional. During the reading of the Scriptures in the order of Malta, the sword should be at "Present Swords" as defined in the Grand Encampment Drill Regulations, and not upward in the right hand.

The Sentinel has no place in Red Cross, Malta or Order of the Temple Asylum Ceremonies. His duty is to take charge of the door, his station being at outside of Asylum Door.

The drawn sword should never at any place in any Order be used as a pointer or in any movement other than those provided in Grand Encampment Drill Regulations.

It is not necessary for the Banner Guards in the Order of Malta to have swords drawn while explaining the banners.

ORDER of the TEMPLE

As the Full Form Opening contains the movements other than the actual conferring of the Order, reference is made thereto, and they are not set out in this explanation.

At page 99, line 20 of Ritual, after the word "Questions," the J. W., will arise, draw sword, salute, march diagonally to position in front of Commander, receive the questions, remain standing until close of line 23, then salute the Commander, about face and go toward the Senior Warden's station and then pass down the South side of Asylum and out Asylum door, not preparation room door.

At page 101, line 10 of Ritual, the J. W., gives battery on the preparation room door. At this door the Warder opens and closes door, but never at the Asylum or Sentinel's door. When the J. W., enters the Asylum at page 101, line 19 of Ritual, he passes up North side of room until about the center, columns right and stops at the center and base of the Triangle, or where the Triangle would be if placed in the center of the Asylum. There he makes his report and at line 26 of same page, he faces right, goes to South side of Asylum, left faces and goes on a direct line to and in front of the Commander's station and presents questions and answers to Commander, then faces about and goes direct to his station, returns sword and is seated.

At page 102, line 15 of Ritual, the J. W., arises, draws sword and salutes and remains at his station until end of Commander's instructions, when he will about face and pass out at preparation room door.

When the J. W., and Pil., enter they should approach the first tent, which should be placed at about the J. W's., station, then the second tent, which should be placed either on the stage in the East, or in the center of the East if there is no stage, then the third tent, which should be at the S. W's, station and then directly to the preparation room door when passsing out.

At page 104, line 8 of Ritual, the battery is given by the J. W., who with the Pil., will wait in preparation room until Escort and Prel., conduct them into the Asylum.

(SEE RITUAL AND PRELATE'S ESCORT FOR DETAILS FOR WORK FOLLOWING THE ABOVE, AND ALSO POSTING OF THE GUARDS.)

Following the obligation and other work, after the S. W., and Pil., have gone out and Guard dismissed, the Triangle will be placed in proper position, and S. W., should then give proper battery on preparation room door and the Ritual, starting on page 108 is followed.

At page 113 of Ritual, when rls., are uncovered, which should be reverently, the pall should not be taken from the Triangle. It should be placed between the bible and the apex of the Triangle, with the cross in full view of the Pil. When once removed, the pall should not be replaced over the rls. In all libations, whenever the Commander goes toward the base of the Triangle, he should go down the South side of it. When escorting P. P., out of the Asylum, S. W. and J. W., should march with swords reversed and the movement in accordance with the Rubric as shown after line 8 on page 116 of Ritual. The work as shown commencing with line 9, page 116 of Ritual should be given at preparation room door unless an actual Sep., is used, and if so, at the Sep. After the Prelate's address, the P. P., will be conducted to the preparation room by the Wardens, who should be at reverse swords and a Triangle movement should be executed if possible. If twelve Sir Knights are used during the first four lib., the Triangle Guard should be placed before the Pil., is brought in and if not, they should be placed at this time. (See Posting of Triangle Guard Ceremony in this Manual.)

The rendition of the remainder of the Order is so clearly explained in the Ritual, that no further elucidation is deemed necessary. The commands during the last lib., should be given by the Sir Knight indicated in the Ritual. It is recommended that the Prelate give lines 10 and 11 on page 124 of Ritual. Explanations and attributes should be given according to Ritual instructions.

PRELATE'S ESCORT

C.:—Sir Knight C. G.: (C. G., rises, draws sword and salutes, Salute Swords) **Form an Escort for the Prelate.** (Ritual 105-11)

C. G.:—1. Sir Knight S. W.: (S. W. rises, advances two paces, draws sword, faces C. G., and salutes) **2. FORM AN ESCORT AND CONDUCT THE PRELATE TO HIS APARTMENT.** (Ritual 105-12)

(S. W. after saluting C. G. will take position in the East, facing West where line is to be formed and command:)

S. W.:—1. Prelate's Escort, 2. ATTENTION, 3. FALL IN.

(The Escort consisting of Sir Knights previously detailed is formed in the South, single file according to height, facing Senior Warden. The S. W., will then take post opposite center of line and command:)

S. W.:—1 Left, 2. FACE, 3. Draw, 4. SWORDS, 5. Count, 6. TWOS, 7. Present, 8. SWORDS.

(Then S. W., about faces, salutes and reports to Prelate.)

S. W.:—Excellent Prelate, the Escort awaits your pleasure.

P.:—(after bowing) **Lead on Sir Knight S. W.** (Slow Movement.)

S. W.:—1. Escort, 2. Carry, 3. SWORDS, 4. Twos right or Right by Twos, 5. MARCH.

(The Escort, with Prelate in rear, passes down North side of Asylum, columns left in West, then right and out Asylum door and is conducted back through the preparation room, where the J. W., and Pil., are in waiting. (Ritual 105-15) The Prelate having received the Candidate as per Ritual, the Escort returns through preparation room door, with the J. W., Prel. and Pil., in the rear of Escort. When inside the Asylum the S. W., commands:)

S. W.:—1. Column right, 2. MARCH, (When near the center of Asylum he commands:) **3. Column left, 4. MARCH, 5. Open order, 6. MARCH, 7. Forward, 8. MARCH.**

(When column has reached about four paces from altar, the S. W., will command:)

S. W.:—1. Escort, 2. HALT, 3. Inward, 4. FACE. (Ritual 105-15.)

(When Prel., and Pil., arrive at foot of lines, (Ritual 105-18) the S. W., will command:)

S. W.:—1. Escort, 2. Present, 3. SWORDS.

(After Prel., Pil., and J. W,, pass through the lines, (Prelate not holding on to Candidate) the S. W., will command:)

S. W.:—1. Escort, 2. Carry, 3. SWORDS.

(After Pil., has been properly placed by J. W., (Crossed swords on top of B.) and Prel., is in position, the S. W., will command:)

S. W.:—1. Sir Knights, 2. Order, 3. SWORDS, 4. UNCOVER. (Ritual 106-3.)

(After obligation and instructions, S. W. and Pil. W., retire as per Rubric at top of page 108 of Ritual. The J. W., having taken post at head of lines, after placing Pil., now takes command of Escort and at line 4, page 107 of Ritual, will command:)

J. W.:—1. Sir Knights, 2. RECOVER, 3. Carry, 4. SWORDS.

(The S. W., and Pil. W., having retired, (Line 23, page 108, Ritual), the J. W., commands:)

J. W.:—1. Escort, 2. Countermarch, 3. Column Right and Left, 4. MARCH.

J. W.:—1. Escort, 2. Column right, 3. MARCH. (and when near the North side of Asylum, continue:) **4. Column right, 5. MARCH, 6. Open order, 7. MARCH, 8. Forward, 9. MARCH, 10. HALT, 11. Inward, 12. FACE, 13. Present, 14. SWORDS.**

(After the Prelate has passed through the lines and resumed his station, he will salute the J. W., who returns the salute and then dismisses the Escort as follows:)

J. W.:—1. Escort, 2. Carry, 3. SWORDS, 4. Return, 5. SWORDS, 6. About, 7. FACE, 8. DISMISSED.

POSTING the GUARD

Order of the Temple.

(The Guard is composed of a certain number of posts, not the Standard Guard, previously designated by numbers. The Pil. is required to pass three guards in this ceremony, therefore, this guard should consist of three posts, one, two, three. The Guard taken as a whole is spoken of as "The Guard," not guards. After the Prelate's Escort has been dismissed, all officers resume their stations and the Commander directs the Captain General to post the Guard as follows:)

C.:—1. Sir Knight C. G.: (Or other designated Officer), 2. POST THE GUARD.

(The C. G., taking station four paces in front of and to the right of Standard Bearer's station, facing to the left, commands:)

C. G.:—1. Guard, 2. FALL IN.

(Three Sir Knights previously designated arrange themselves in column of files, three paces from and facing the C. G., who commands:)

C. G.:—1. Left, 2. FACE, 3. Draw, 4. SWORDS, 5. COUNT OFF.

(The guards then count from right to left, one, two, three. The C. G., then takes station three paces in front of and facing the center, or No. 2 guard. As the Pil., must give the P. W. W., to all three guards and great care should be given that this is properly communicated, consequently the entire guard must receive the word. The C. G., then commands:)

C. G.:—1. Guard Number Two.

(Number two guard steps forward one pace and halts directly in front of the C. G., who commands:)

C. G.:—1. GUARD, (C. G. and Guard assume position of Guard together), 2. Give CUTS, 3. COMMUNICATE TO ME THE P. W. W. (Word Communicated.), 4. Carry, 5. SWORDS, 6. POST. (Guard executes about face and resumes post in line.)

C. G.:—1. Guard, 2. Right, 3. FACE, 4. Forward, 5. MARCH.

(The C. G., then marches the guard in column of files across in front of Standard Guard, up the North side of Asylum to near Northeast corner which is designated as Post No. 1, where he will command:)

C. G.:—1. Guard, 2. HALT, 3. Number one, 4. POST.

(Number one guard will side step out of line to position and the C. G., will then instruct him as follows:)

C. G.:—Number one, take charge of this post and allow none to pass except such as are qualified and have the Word.

(Number one salutes, which is answered by the C. G. The guard then steps forward so that number two is on line with the C. G., who marches them across front of Asylum and posts number two in the same manner near the southeast corner and then posts number three in the same manner in the center of the south side of the Asylum. The C. G., then takes post in center of the Asylum, facing the Commander and reports:)

C. G.:—Eminent Commander, the guard is posted.

(Commander acknowledges salute without comment. C. G., then returns to his station. The S. W. accompanied by the Pil., enters at the preparation room door, goes up North side of Asylum, then across the East, then down the South side, then across to North side and turns left and out preparation room door, the cuts and word having been given to each guard at his post. After the S. W. and Pil., have passed out of the Asylum, the C. G., reports to the Commander as follows:)

C. G.:—Eminent Commander, the guard duty has been performed.

C.:—1. Sir Knight C. G., 2. DISMISS THE GUARD.

(The C. G., then marches from his station to Post Number One and commands as follows:)

C. G.:—1. Number one, 2. FALL IN, and then passing on to number two and three directs them to fall in in the same manner, they doing so behind number one according to number. The C. G., then marches them to place where originally formed and commands:)

C. G.:—1. HALT.

(C. G., then executes a Left Face and places himself in front of Guard and commands:)

C. G.:—1. Guard, 2. Return, 3. SWORDS, 4. DISMISSED.

(The C. G., then returns to his station and reports to Commander as follows:)

C. G.:—Eminent Commander, your order has been obeyed.

(Commander acknowledges the salute of C. G., and the C. G., then takes his seat)

(The above plan may be used in posting the Hermits if desired, but titles must be changed.)

POSTING the TRIANGLE GUARD

Order Of The Temple

(The Officers being in their stations, the Commander will command:)

C.:—1. Sir Knight C. G., 2. FORM AND POST THE TRANGLE GUARD.

(C. G., Hand salutes and proceeds to point on line with and in front of Recorder's station, facing West, and draws sword.

C. G.:—1. Triangle Guard, 2. FALL IN.

(The six Sir Knights previously detailed for this duty, immediately fall in, facing East.)

C. G.:—1. Left, 2. FACE, 3. Draw, 4. SWORDS, 5. Count, 6. TWOS, 7. Triangle Guard, 8. Twos, right, 9. MARCH, 10. Column left, 11. MARCH, (and as head

of column arrives on line with the Commander, wil
command) 12. **Column left**, 13. **MARCH**, (and as hea(
of column arrives one pace from apex of Triangle, wil
command) 14. **Divisions**, 15. **Columns half right an(
left**, 16. **MARCH**, (and as head of column arrives on(
pace from base of triangle, will command:) 17. **Tri
angle Guard**, 18. **HALT**, 19. **Inward**, 20. **FACE.**

(The C. G., then faces the Commander, who is in th(
East, and reports:)

C. G.:—**Eminent Commander, the Triangle Guar(
is formed and posted.** (C. G., then takes his station.)

THE STANDARD GUARD

The Grand Standard is not a parade banner an(
is recommended never to be carried in public parades.

(NOTE—**It is permissible to carry the Gran(
Standard on Church Parade, or better, it may be de
mounted and set up in the church.**)

For public parade the Colors consist of a Nationa
Flag, and the Beauseant.

For Asylum use only the Beauseant may be car
ried.

(For description of the Grand Standard and Beau
seant, see G. E. Constitution and Statutes, Section Nos
238 and 239.)

The Beauseant will salute with the Commander)
at all commands to present swords, and at other time(
as provided. (The above applies only when the Beau
seant is being carried, or in the hands of a Sir Knigh(
of the Standard Guard.)

**THE NATIONAL FLAG NEVER RENDERS OF
ACKNOWLEDGES ANY SALUTE.**

If marching, the salute with the Beauseant is ex
ecuted when six paces from the officer; the carry is re
sumed when six paces beyond him.

Colors are said to be "cased" when furled and pro
tected by a covering.

In the Asylum the Grand Standard and Beausean(
shall be displayed in the West in line with the chair(
of the Sword Bearer and Standard Bearer, the Beau
seant being on the right of the Warder and the Gran(
Standard on the right of the Standard Bearer.

The Sword Bearer commands the Standard Guard
marches on its right, and does not carry a flag or ban

ner, and when in command and giving commands, should always have his sword drawn.

In Asylum movements, the Beauseant is carried by the Standard Bearer, who marches in the center of the Standard Guard. The Warder should march as do other Sir Knights in the ranks, and generally at Carry Swords.

For Parade movements outside of the Asylum, the U. S. Flag is carried by the Standard Bearer and the Beauseant by the Warder and the U. S. Flag should always be on the right or at the head of the column, or other banners carried.

KNIGHT TEMPLAR TITLES AND THEIR USE.

The honorary title of the Grand Master is "Most Eminent," and the official title is "Grand Master."

The honorary title of each of the other officers is "Right Eminent."

The honorary title shall be used in addressing or referring to an officer, and when so used shall immediately precede the official title, e. g.: "Most Eminent Grand Master, Right Eminent Grand Treasurer," etc. The official title only shall be used by an officer when necessary to designate his rank or official station. (Section 31, Grand Encampment Constitution.)

The honorary title of the Grand Commander is "Right Eminent," and his official title is "Grand Commander." The honorary title of the Deputy Grand Commander is "Very Eminent," and his official title is "Deputy Grand Commander." The honorary title of the remaining officers of a Grand Commandery is "Eminent."

The honorary title shall be used when an officer is addressed and shall immediately precede the official title, thus: "Right Eminent Grand Commander, Very Eminent Deputy Grand Commander, Eminent Grand Senior Warden." When referring to an officer, the honorary title shall immediately follow the name, thus: "Sir Knight John Doe, Right Eminent Grand Commander; Sir Knight James Brown, Very Eminent Deputy Grand Commander; Sir Knight Peter Roe, Eminent Grand Senior Warden." The official title shall be used by an officer only when necessary to designate his rank or official station, thus: "I am Sir Knight John Jones, Grand Commander." (Section 54, Grand Encampment Constitution.)

The honorary title of the Commander is "Eminent," and the official title is "Commander."

The honorary title of all other officers and individual members of the Order is "Sir Knight."

The honorary title shall be used in addressing or referring to an officer, and when so used shall immediately precede the official title, e. g.: "Eminent Commander, Sir Knight Captain General, Sir Knight Warder," etc.

The title of each and every Knight Templar, when addressed or referred to by either or both his Christian and surname is "Sir Knight," without any prefix thereto, and "Sir Knights" is the title to be applied to any assemblage of Knights Templar.

Retention Of Rank

Section 235 of the Grand Encampment Constitution provides as follows:

"One who has filled by installation and term of service, the office of Grand Master, Deputy Grand Master, Grand Generalissimo or Grand Captain General in the Grand Encampment; Grand Commander, Deputy Grand Commander, Grand Generalissimo or Grand Captain General in a Grand Commandery; or Commander in a Commandery; shall retain the title of the highest office attained by him in the Grand Encampment, Grand Commandery and Commandery, with the word, "Past" immediately preceding and qualifying the official title. Past rank is limited to the offices named in this section. For example, Sir Knight Joseph Kyle Orr, Most Eminent Past Grand Master, Sir Knight John Fishel, Eminent Past Commander.

In other words there is no change from an actual holder of an office, as set out above, save prefixing the word "Past" immediately preceding and qualifying the official title.

HONORS AND SALUTES.

National Anthem and National Flag.

The composition consisting of the words and music known as the "Star Spangled Banner" is designated the National Anthem of the United States of America.

At all parades and ceremonies under arms, the commandery will render the prescribed salute and will remain in the position of salute while the National Anthem is being played.

If not under arms, the commandery will be brought to attention at the first note of the National Anthem, or To The Color, and the salute rendered by the officer in command.

When the National Anthem is played at any place where Sir Knights are present, all not in formation will stand at attention facing toward the music, saluting with the right hand; if the National Flag is present they will face toward it.

If in civilian clothes, covered, they will uncover at the first note of the Anthem, holding the head dress over the left breast with the right hand, and so remain until its close, except that in inclement weather the head dress may be slightly raised. If uncovered, they will salute with the hand, at the first note of the Anthem, retaining the position of salute until the last note.

The same rules apply when To The Color is sounded as when the National Anthem is played.

The National Anthem shall be played through without repetition of any part not required to be repeated to make it complete.

The playing of the National Anthem as part of a medley is prohibited.

Sir Knights not in formation will on all occasions salute the National Flag when carried by a body authorized by law or regulation to carry it.

When the National Flag passes a commandery or subdivision of Knights they will be brought to attention and the Commander and officers will salute.

Officers, only will salute while marching in formation. The Knights will be at carry swords when marching honors are given.

In rendering honors the commandery or subdivision will be faced to the front; they will not present swords when facing to a flank.

All Sir Knights not in formation passing the uncovered National Flag, or when the National Flag passes, will render honors as follows: If in uniform and sword drawn they will salute with the sword; if in uniform, covered or uncovered, with the hand salute; if in civilian dress and covered, they will uncover, holding the head dress over the left breast with the right hand; if uncovered, they will salute with the hand salute.

All hand salutes are given with the right hand.

Every National Flag in a passing Templar parade will be saluted.

No honors are paid when on route marches.

No salutes are rendered when marching in double time.

A mounted Sir Knight dismounts before addressing an officer not mounted.

A mounted officer dismounts before addressing a superior officer not mounted.

When several officers in company are saluted, all who are entitled to the salute return it.

OFFICIAL KNIGHT TEMPLAR HONORS

The honors to be paid by Templars, beyond true knightly courtesy, are such as are due to the official position held by such officers.

The Grand Master is saluted with highest honors; all standards and banners dropping, officers and Sir Knights saluting, bands, trumpets, or field music, sounding "President's March."

The Deputy Grand Master is received with standards and banners dropping, officers and Sir Knights saluting, bands, trumpets or field music, sounding "General's March."

All other officers of the Grand Encampment, and a Grand Commander, within his own grand jurisdiction, are received with standards and banners dropping, officers and Sir Knights saluting, trumpets sounding three flourishes.

A Grand Commander, outside his own grand jurisiction, is received with standards and banners droping, officers and Sir Knights saluting, trumpets sounding two flourishes.

A Deputy Grand Commander, the Grand Generalissimo, the Grand Captain General and Past Grand Commanders, within their own grand jurisdictions, re received with standards and banners dropping, officers and Sir Knights saluting, trumpets sounding two ourishes. Outside of their own jurisdictions they are ntitled to but one flourish.

All other grand officers, within their own grand urisdictions, are received with standards and banners ropping, officers and Sir Knights saluting, trumpets ounding one flourish. Outside their own grand jurisiction the flourish is omitted.

An Eminent Commander is saluted by his own ommandery with standards and banners dropping, officers and Sir Knights saluting, trumpets sounding one ourish. Outside of his own commandery he is not entitled to the flourish. The officer commanding a battaon is entitled to the same salute.

Jewels Of Office, And How Worn.

All officers of the Grand Encampment, of Grand ommanderies, and of Subordinate and Constitutent ommanderies shall wear the jewel of their respective ffice during incumbency in office. (G. E. Reg. Sec. 56.)

Only Templar Jewels are to be worn on the Templar uniform, Meritorius Jewels, Badge of Commanderes and Malta Jewel may be worn on the left breast, laced in the order named, on a line with the third button of the coat. (G. E. Reg. Sec. 257.)

The style and manner of wearing jewels is fully xplained in Sections 258 to 262 inclusive of the Contitution and Statutes of the Grand Encampment of he United States of America; also Emblem of the rder and Knights Templar Button, Sections 263 and 64 of the same Regulations.

Rank At Parades.

(While the above topic applies mainly in outdoor

movements, it also has some application to Asylum movements, and therefore, is included in this Manual.)

When several Commanders parade together, they take rank according to the date of their respective charters, unless they voluntarily waive such rank. Courtesy and Templar usage, however, may accord some particular Commandery a place on the right of the line or column, in the nature of an escort to the others.

If the Grand Commander or other Grand Officer entitled to command be not present, the Commander of the senior Commandery may assume command.

As far as possible, Commanderies should form for parade in column of threes, sections or divisions, right in front and the Standard Guard forming one of the files of three.

A Commandery shall appear in public only in full dress uniform. (G. E. Stat. Sec. 216.)

For parades and escorts of honor, where two or more Commanderies act together, a competent officer should be selected as Marshal for the occasion, whose commands shall be obeyed and repeated to each Commandery in line by the proper officers. Commanderies are stationed in line in the order of their number, except that the escorting Commandery will take the left of the line until the column is ready to move, when the Captain General of the escorting Commandery will command:

Captain General:—1. Right by threes, 2. MARCH: after five paces: 3. Column right, 4. MARCH, passing the lines of the other Commanderies, Knights at CARRY swords, Commander and Generalissimo at SECURE swords, Captain General at SALUTE swords; Beauseant dipped.

Escorts Of Honor

Escorts of Honor are rarely used in the ordinary Commandery and as they are fully explained in the current Grand Encampment Drill Regulations, Section 158, reference is made thereto and where it is necessary to form an Escort of Honor, the Drill Regulations should be complied with.

THE UNITED STATES FLAG

The Grand Encampment at its 1934 Triennial Conclave adopted the following:

"All Commanderies in the United States of America, including its territories and dependencies, shall display a silk regulation flag of the United States in their respective Asylums, to be placed on the dais at the extreme right."

This means that the flag must be placed on the dais or raised platform, under no circumstances farther back than the Commander or Presiding Officer; on his right and near the edge of the dais or platform, and must so remain at all times when the Conclave is in session, unless the Ritual provides otherwise.

At the Grand Encampment Conclave held at Miami in 1937 a new Flag Lecture was adopted and is shown at page 129 of Ritual; also manner of displaying the Flag while the lecture is given at page 128 of Ritual. This is mandatory. After the Commander has directed the Standard Bearer to "Display the U. S. Flag," and while making the explanation, Sir Knights in uniform and with arms, will comply with the commands of the Commander. Sir Knights not in uniform will stand at attention. THE UNITED STATES FLAG IS NEVER MARCHED TO THE REAR.

THE NATIONAL FLAG

In decorating with the National Flag, never festoon or drape it. Hang it flat. If hung so stripes are horizontal, union should be in the left upper corner. If hung perpendicularly, union should be in the left upper corner. When carried in parades or crossed with other flags, the National Flag should always be on the right.

The National Flag should never be placed below a person sitting.

INSIGNIA OF RANK AND SHOULDER STRAPS

Section 246 of the Constitution and Statutes of the Grand Encampment of Knights Templar of the United States of America as Enacted in 1934, provides as follows:

"All officers shall wear on their uniforms the insignia of Rank, and on their Templar dress coats the Shoulder Straps, to denote the rank attained or office held, and no member shall wear the emblem described in Section 241 or the Shoulder Straps described in Sections 242 to 244 inclusive unless he shall have attained the rank or shall hold the office which the wearing of such emblems or Shoulder Straps denotes."

PRELATE'S AND CEREMONIAL ROBES

The Prelate's robe is strictly under the jurisdiction of the Grand Encampment and is fully set out in Sections 253 and 254 of the 1934 Constitution of the Grand Encampment, Section 254 prescribing when same may be worn.

Section 255 provides that the Ceremonial Robes, dress and equipment of the Illustrious Order of the Red Cross and of the Knight of Malta shall be as prescribed in the Ritual.

JEWELS OF OFFICE, EMBLEM OF THE ORDER AND KNIGHT TEMPLAR BUTTON, are fully covered in Sections 256 to 264, inclusive of the Grand Encampment Constitution of 1934.

INSIGNIA OF RANK AND SHOULDER STRAPS are fully explained, and their use defined in Sections 241 to 246, inclusive, of the Constitution of the Grand Encampment of 1934.

KNIGHT TEMPLAR UNIFORMS.

Specifications for Knight Templar Uniforms, both Dress and Fatigue, are set out in full in the 1938 Annual Report of the Grand Commandery of Minnesota.

CHRISTMAS DAY SERVICES

The Knights, without uniform, will assemble in their Asylum about one hour previous to the official time of toast, which in Minnesota is 11 o'clock A. M., Central Standard time.

Tables will be set, in some dignified and pleasing manner, and a glass provided for each Sir Knight present. It will add to beauty of the occasion if the Sir Knights form in procession, two abreast and march in to the Asylum, a line on each side of the tables, the officers at the front and all take their positions, and at the sound of the gavel, all will be seated.

Families of the Sir Knights and Masonic Brethren and their families, may be in attendance, but only the Sir Knights at the tables can participate in the toasts and ceremonies.

The services should open with some appropriate music, either by a choir, a soloist or by all present. Music such as "Hark! the Herald Angels Sing!" should be used. The following service is then followed:

Commander:—Excellent Prelate read us a lesson from the Holy Scriptures.

Now when Jesus was born in Bethlehem of Judea in the days of Herod the King, behold, there came wise men from the east to Jerusalem.

Saying, Where is he that is born King of the Jews? for we have seen his star in the east, and are come to worship him.

When Herod the King had heard these things, he was troubled, and all Jerusalem with him.

And when he had gathered all the chief priests and scribes of the people together, he demanded of them where Christ should be born.

And they said unto him, In Bethlehem of Judea; for thus it is written by the prophet.

And thou Bethlehem, in the land of Juda; art not the least among the princes of Juda: for out of thee shall come a Governor that shall rule my people Isreal.

Then Herod, when he had privily called the wise men, enquired of them diligently what time the star appeared.

And he sent them to Bethlehem, and said, Go and search diligently for the young child; and when ye have found him, bring me word again, that I may come and worship him also.

When they had heard the king, they departed; and, lo, the star, which they saw in the east, went before them, till it came and stood over where the young child was.

When they saw the star, they rejoiced with exceeding great joy.

And when they were come into the house, they saw the young child with Mary his mother, and fell down, and worshipped him: and when they had opened their treasures, they presented unto him gifts; gold, and frankincense, and myrrh. Matthew 2:1-11.

And there were in the same country shepherds abiding in the field, keeping watch over their flock by night.

And lo, the angel of the Lord came upon them, and the glory of the Lord shone around about them; and they were sore afraid. And the angel said unto them, Fear not; for behold, I bring you good tidings of great joy, which shall be to all people. For unto you is born this day in the city of David a Savior, which is Christ the Lord * * And suddenly there was with the angel a multitude of the heavenly host praising God, and saying,

CHOIR OR SIR KNIGHTS. Glory to God in the highest, and on earth peace, good will toward men. (Luke 2:8-14.)

Appropriate Music

Commander:— Sir Knights, on this glorious day we commemorate the birth of Jesus of Nazareth, Emmanuel, author of our salvation, and the Great Captain under whose banner we have all enlisted.

On this day, nineteen hundred and_____ _____years ago, there was born in Bethlehem of Judea one who laid aside the God-head, and assumed mortal flesh; one whose glory, worth and grace no language can express, one who was born that our lives might be purified, and who died that our souls might be redeemed from the penalty of sin.

Let us, as true Soldiers of the Cross, strive to profit by the birth, life, death, resurrection and ascension of that Divine Master, and remain his faithful soldiers unto death. Seeking strength to continue that struggle, let us now accompany our Prelate to the throne of heavenly grace.

Excellent Prelate, lead our devotions, Sir Knights, ATTENTION.

(All fold arms and bow heads.)

Prelate-Almighty God, Father of all mercies, we do give Thee most humble and hearty thanks for all Thy goodness and loving kindness to us and to all men. We Bless Thee for our creation, preservation, and all the blessings of this life, but above all, for Thine inestimable love in the redemption of the world by our Lord Jesus Christ; for the means of grace and for the hope of glory. And, we beseech Thee give us that due sense of all Thy mercies, that our hearts may be unfeignedly thankful, and that we show forth Thy praise, not only with our lips but in our lives, by giving up ourselves to Thy service, and by walking before Thee in holiness and righteousness all our days.

Have mercy, we beseech Thee, upon this whole land; and so rule the hearts of Thy servants, the President of the United States, the Governors of all States, and all others in authority, that they knowing whose ministers they are, may above all things seek Thy honor and glory; and that we and all the people, duly considering whose authority they bear, may faithfully and obediently honor them in Thee, and for Thee, according to Thy blessed Word and ordinance.

We remember, O Lord, and we beseech Thee to remember, all the lawfully constituted bodies of our Order, the Grand Encampment of the United States of America, and all our Commanderies, Grand, Constituent and Subordinate. Bless them with peace, prosperity and piety, and direct them in all their doings, with Thy most gracious favor, that in all their works, they may glorify Thy Holy Name, and finally by Thy mercy obtain everlasting life.

We beseech Thee to remember all the Officers of our Order, and especially the Grand Master and Officers of the Grand Encampment of the United States of America the Grand Commander and other Officers of the Grand Commandery of Minnesota, and the Commanders and other Officers of the Commanderies here assembled in Thy name and presence. May the words of their mouths, and the meditations of their hearts, and the actions of their lives, be always acceptable in Thy sight.

We remember, O Lord, and we beseech Thee to remember, all the members of this Order, and the faithful Brethren and Companions of all other Masonic Orders, wheresoever dispersed throughout the world. Look upon the sick and the afflicted with the eyes of Thy mercy, comfort them with a sense of Thy goodness; preserve them from the temptations of the enemy, lift up Thy countenance upon them and give them peace. Bless the well in their lying down and in their rising up, in their going out and in their coming in. Fill Thou their basket and their store. Go with them in their journeyings. Abide with all whom they may leave behind, so that, in joy returning, they may find their own in peace, remaining, with a grateful sense of Thy mercies. This we ask through Jesus Christ our Lord. Amen.

Commander:—Sir Knights (they drop hands and raise heads.) BE SEATED.

(If it is desired to start toasts exactly on the hour, silence may be maintained or they may have the freedom of the time for conversation, but should not leave their seats. If this is done the Commander will sound his gavel at the time he desires to proceed.)

TOAST TO THE GRAND MASTER

Commander:—Sir Knight Recorder, read the sentiment.

Recorder:—(Reads sentiment as supplied to Commanderies.)

Commander:—(On the first stroke of the hour.) To our Grand Master! Partake.

Sir Knights:—(Repeat.) "To our Grand Master." (And partake.)

Commander:—Sir Knight Recorder, read the Grand Master's response.

Recorder:—(Reads the response.)

TOAST TO THE GRAND COMMANDER

Commander:—Sir Knight Recorder, read the sentiment of the Grand Commander.

Recorder:—(Reads sentiment, if any.)

Commander:—To the Grand Commander of Knights Templar of Minnesota.

Sir Knights: (Repeat.) To the Grand Commander of Knights Templar of Minnesota, (And partake.)

Commander:—Sir Knight Recorder, read the Grand Commander's response.

Recorder:—(Reads the response, if any.)

(At this point it is advisable to have an address, with music both before and after the address.)

OTHER TOASTS.

Commander:—To all Knights Templar, wherever dispersed.

Sir Knights:—(Repeat.) To all Knights Templar, wherever dispersed. (And partake.)

Commander:—To all Knights Templar who have shed their blood in defense of Liberty and Christianity.

Sir Knights:—(Repeat, then bow their heads in silence; no drinking.)

Commander:—To the Grand Master of Royal and Select Masters of Minnesota.

Sir Knights:—(Repeat.) To the Grand Master of Royal and Select Masters of Minn. (And partake.)

Commander:—To the Grand High Priest of Royal Arch Masons of Minnesota.

Sir Knights:—(Repeat.) To the Grand High Priest of Royal Arch Masons of Minnesota. (And partake.)

Commander:—To the Grand Master of Masons of Minnesota.

Sir Knights:—(Repeat.) To the Grand Master of Masons of Minnesota. (And partake.)

Commander:—In memory of the dead of this jurisdiction during the year 19____. (All present will bow their heads, while in soft tones, a hymn such as "Nearer, My God, to Thee," will be sung.)

Commander:—Sir Knights, ATTENTION. We have been refreshed by these hallowed memories; now let us receive the benediction of our Excellent Prelate.

Prelate:—May the Lord bless thee and keep thee; may the Lord make his face to shine upon thee and be gracious unto thee; may the Lord lift up his countenance upon thee, and give thee peace. Amen.

Commander:—(Sound the gavel.)   Sir Knights. You are dismissed.

(Responses may be made to some or all of the toasts when offered, but it is advisable not to have too many responses.)

EASTER SERVICE

"Christ the Lord is risen today,
Sons of men and angels say:
Raise your joys and triumphs high,
Sing, ye heavens, and earth reply."

Perhaps the above verse proclaims, as strongly as possible, just what the character of the Easter Service should be. A day and service of Joy and Gladness. This, we believe, can best be accomplished by a service made up of a sermon or inspirational address, interspersed with Anthems, Hymns and Choruses, commemorative of the day.

Attendance at some place of worship will probably enable the average Commandery to more fully enjoy the day than by a service in their own Asylum. Most any church will welcome a Commandery at their service, and if their accommodations are not large enough to handle their own membership and the Sir Knights at their regular service, the Pastor will undoubtedly make arrangements for a special service at some other hour of the day, convenient to all parties. An effort should be made to attend different churches each year, if possible, so no question of denomination or creed can be raised.

Our Order is based on the Christian Religion and the practice of the Christian Virtues and we should not be ashamed to acknowledge to the world just what we stand for, and we believe that church attendance is an open acknowledgement to the world that we are proud and sincere in our belief and of our Order, and wish to openly and with dignity carry our banners in the cause and defense of the Christian Religion.

When the Commandery does attend church service, the parade, entrance and departure should be in accordance with instructions set out in this Manual, with reference to other church appearances.

When the service is in the Asylum of the Commandery, the sword should not be worn. Entrance and departure should be in a dignified manner, chapeau may either be removed and placed on right shoulder on entering, or may be left on until the Sir Knights seat themselves, and if so should be in unison.

FUNERAL CEREMONIES

(Funeral Ceremonies must be distinguished from Funeral Escorts and Funeral Service.)

(If a Commandery is conducting a Funeral Service, the ceremony as adopted by the Grand Encampment must be followed. The latest service at the present time was that adopted at Minneapolis in 1931. The General Regulations, Ritualistic Work, Formations, Commands, etc., are so fully set out and explained in the Knight Templar Funeral Service as published under the authority of the Grand Encampment that but little additional explanation is necessary. Mention is also made of the title "Church Parade," as shown at page 62 of the present Drill Regulations of the Grand Encampment, which have been adopted in its present form, and as it may be amended in the future.)

All commands should be given in a dignified and subdued manner and especially if the service is to be held at a church, the conduct of all Sir Knights should be as dignified as it would be on attending Church under any other circumstance.

If the Commandery is conducting the service itself, it should be opened in full or short form and at the proper time arrive at the place where the service will be held, which should not be far enough in advance of the time to permit the Sir Knights to break out of line or to smoke or do other things that you would not do attending a church service. After conducting the service and on return to the Asylum, the Commandery must be closed in regular form.

In attending any service at a Church, whether Funeral, Easter, Christmas, Palm Sunday, Ascension Sunday, or any other Church appearance, the Commandery, after the U. S. Flag and Beauseant has been placed at the right and left of chancel respectively, will march in in column of files, at SECURE SWORDS and with CHAPEAU REMOVED BY RIGHT HAND AND PLACED ON LEFT SHOULDER. THE SAME PROCEDURE WILL BE FOLLOWED ON LEAVING

THE CHURCH. THIS IS THE ONLY TIME AND PLACE THAT THE CHAPEAU IS REMOVED BY THE RIGHT HAND AND PLACED ON THE LEFT SHOULDER. IF IT IS A FUNERAL SERVICE CONDUCTED AT THE GRAVE BY THE COMMANDERY THE CHAPEAU IS REMOVED BY THE LEFT HAND AND PLACED ON THE RIGHT SHOULDER.

The Sword, Chapeau and Templar Cross must be on the casket during the entire service, and is only removed at the close of the service at the grave. If it is not possible to keep the sword, cross and chapeau on the casket during the procession from the place of first service to the cemetery, the Captain General should see that either the mortician takes them to the cemetery or do so himself. Some families prefer that the sword and chapeau be placed on the casket, while it may be lying in state and this may be done only in cases where the Commandery conducts the service.

If the Commandery conducts the service, it is advisable that the Prelate wear the robes of his office, but if it is only an escort, he should wear his Templar uniform.

It is preferable, especially in cold or inclement weather, to give the major portion of the Ritualistic Work in the Asylum, Church or Home, wherever the first part of the ceremony is being held.

If the Asylum, Church or Home is sufficiently large to permit of placing all the Sir Knights either in the rear or at ends of casket, or in both places, thus leaving a clear view of the casket to the audience, this is advisable. This same procedure or formation is also advised for the ceremonies at the grave.

FUNERAL ESCORT

If the Commandery is requested to act as Escort at a Funeral where the ceremony is conducted by a Lodge or other Masonic Body, the following form may be used. If some part of the service is not given by a Masonic Body, no escort can be furnished. It is not necessary to open a Commandery if only an escort is to be furnished.

The Commandery will be formed, preferably in column of twos, if the conditions will permit; with sword hilts draped. The Commander and Generalissimo should be in front, then Past Commanders according to seniority, followed by the other officers and Sir Knights. The Captain General will be in command at all times. Should the ceremony be held in the Asylum, at the proper time the Captain General will report to the Master of the Lodge that the escort is in readiness, and when all is ready, will march into the Asylum, followed by the Lodge. If the Asylum, (or other place used, will permit, it is advisable to take position in a line or lines across the room, at head of casket, leaving room for the Lodge to form in front of the Commandery and also at head of casket. Where there is a stage it may be used in placing the Commandery. If at a church or home where room will not permit, the placing of both the Lodge and the Commandery, the Commandery may open ranks and allow the Lodge to pass through and remain outside, or go into the place individually but must be in position to escort the Lodge when it comes out. If the service is held at a church, the Sir Knights should enter at Secure Swords, with chapeau removed by Right Hand and placed on Left Shoulder. If at Asylum or Home, the Commandery should enter at Secure Swords but chapeau is not removed.

All commands should be given by the Captain General in a dignified and subdued manner. After entering and taking positions, the swords should be dropped to side, and at all Prayers, the chapeau should be removed and placed on right shoulder.

At the close of the service the Lodge should stand fast until the Commandery passes out, which should be done the same as on entering, that is by column of twos, one on either side of Lodge and Casket.

Practically the same formations may be made at the grave, with the exception that the Commandery should open ranks and allow the Lodge to pass through then take position behind Lodge, whether in lines at sides or head of grave. It is also advisable not to break ranks after ceremony at grave until after having marched near the conveyances if riding, or a reasonable distance if marching.

FUNERAL SERVICE

(The Knights Templar Funeral Service is direct
ly under the supervision of the Grand Encampmen
and the service prescribed must be used.)

GENERAL REGULATIONS

Every Knight Templar who was in regular stand
ing at the time of his death is entitled to be buriec
with the funeral honors of Knighthood. An unaffiliat
ed Knight Templar is not entitled of right to sucł
honors but a Commandery may grant them to hin
without breach of knightly duty.

Upon notice of the death of a Sir Knight entitlec
to funeral honors and upon his previous request or the
request of his family, it is the duty of the Commander
to convene his Commandery for the purpose of attend
ing the ceremonies.

The Sir Knights will wear the Templar Dress Uni
form, their sword hilts being suitably draped in mourn
ing. In inclement weather the Templar Fatigue Uni
form with or without swords, may be worn and un
covering may be omitted. If the Standard Guard be
present with the Colors the latter shall be furled anc
draped in mourning.

A small Templar cross should be placed on the cas
ket. The chapeau, and sword in scabbard, and, if the
frater was an officer, his jewel trimmed with crape
shall also be placed there.

To receive and escort the remains to the place de
signated for the service, the Commandery will march ir
the usual order of parades, preferably in charge of the
Captain General with the Commander and staff, in
cluding the Prelate, wearing his Robes of Office, anc
the Honor Guard, marching at the head. On arrival
the line will be formed opposite and facing the hearse
The Commander will pass to the front into the home
or funeral parlor and report for duty. The Honor
Guard (six Sir Knights under command of one of
their number) will precede the casket and later marcł
at the side of the hearse. As the casket appears the
Captain General will command; 1, Present, 2. SWORDS

He will then face front and assume the position of salute swords. When the casket has been placed in the hearse, he will resume the carry, face about and command: 1. Carry, 2. SWORDS. He will then form column of threes and proceed to the front of the column, behind the Police escort and musicians if they are present. The Commander and staff will follow the Commandery and precede the hearse. The Sir Knights will march at reverse swords and the Commander and staff at secure swords.

As the procession arrives at the place designated to hold the service, the Commandery will resume carry swords, form a line as before facing the place where the hearse will be halted, and execute the present swords as the casket is being removed and placed upon the carriage. They will then return swords and march in a column of files into the chapel, asylum or burial place uncovering at the door if it is a Church and remaining so while within the Church, preferably remaining at the south side of the bier and retaining their formation so as to be able to leave in the same formation. The Commander and staff, who have followed the column will take position at the head of the bier or in the East and Wardens at the foot of the bier.

The casket is brought in and placed upon the bier, the Guard of Honor, at carry swords, being on either side. The family and friends are seated on the north side of the bier. When all is in readiness the Honor Guard will form the arch of steel over the casket.

No fixed rules are possible as changing conditions are the governing factors. If the service is to be wholly at the cemetery, the "bier" will become the "grave." No provisions are made for seating the participants in this Ceremony but this can be done by the Captain General, in which event he will bring the Commandery to "Attention" before the reading of Scripture lessons or Prayer.

Preferably the larger part of the funeral service is rendered at the house of the deceased, at a church or at some place of public assembly, but the entire rites may be given at the grave.

The service will be conducted according to the following ritual.

(NOTE: The Guard of Honor may be used at the house or at the public place of assembly, and if used will cross swords over the casket at the beginning of the service.)

All being in readiness the choir may render an appropriate selection.

RITUAL.

EMINENT COMMANDER:—Sir Knights, in the solemn ceremonies of our Order, we have often been reminded of the great truth that we are born to die. The mournful funeral knell has betokened that another spirit has winged its flight to a new state of existence. An alarm has come to the door of our asylum, the messenger is Death; and none presumes to say to the direful presence, "Who dares approach?" A Pilgrim Warrior has been summoned, "and there is no discharge in that war." A burning taper in the life of onr Commandery has been extinguished and none save the High and Holy One can relight it.

The earthly remains of our beloved frater lie mute before us and the light of the eye and the breathing of the lips in their language of fraternal greeting have ceased for us forever on this side of the grave. His sword vowed to be drawn only in the cause of truth, justice and liberty, reposes in its scabbard and our arms can no more shield him from wrong or oppression.

(If the Guard of Honor is used at the house or at the public place of assembly its members will here execute Carry Swords and Order Swords at a signal from the Commander but they remain standing at the sides of the casket.)

It is meet, at such a time, that we should be silent, and let the words of the Infinite and Undying speak, that we may gather consolation from His revelation, impress upon our minds lessons from His wisdom and learn the meetness of preparation for the last great change which must come upon us all.

Let us be reverently attentive while the Prelate reads to us a lesson from the Holy Scriptures.

CAPTAIN GENERAL:—1. Un, 2. COVER.

(The following passages of Scriptures or some portions therefore shall then be read.)

PRELATE:

"Lord, Thou hast been our dwelling place in all generations.

Before the mountains were brought forth or ever Thou hadst formed the earth or the world, even from everlasting to everlasting, Thou art God. So teach us to number our days that we may get us an heart of wisdom.

"Bless the Lord, O my soul, and all that is within me—Bless His Holy Name.

Bless the Lord, O my soul, and forget not all His benefits.

Who forgiveth all Thine iniquities, who healeth all Thy diseases. Who redeemeth Thy life from destruction. Who crowneth Thee with loving kindness and tender mercies.

"Like, as a father pitieth his children, so the Lord pitieth them that fear Him, for He knoweth our frame. He remembereth that we are dust.

As for man, his days are as grass. As a flower of the field so he flourisheth, for the wind passeth over it and it is gone, and the place thereof shall know it no more.

But the mercy of the Lord is from everlasting to everlasting, upon them that fear him, and his righteousness to children's children to such as keep his covernant and to those that remember his precepts to do them.

"The Spirit Himself beareth witness with our spirits that we are children of God, and if children of God, then heirs of God and joint heirs of Christ, if so be that we suffer with Him that we may be also glorified with Him. For I reckon that the sufferings of this time are not worthy to be compared with the glory which shall be revealed to us.

"If God is for us, who is against us. He that spared not His own son, but delivered him up for us all, how shall He not also with Him really give us all things. And who shall separate us from the love of

Christ? Shall tribulation or anguish or persecution or famine or nakedness or peril or sword. Nay, in all these things we are more than conquerors through Him that loved us.

For I am persuaded that neither death nor life, nor angels nor principalities, nor things present, nor things to come, nor powers, nor height, nor depth, nor any other creature shall be able to separate us from the love of God which is in Christ Jesus, our Lord.

"But now hath Christ been raised from the dead, the first fruits of them that are asleep. For since by man came death, by man came also the resurrection of the dead. For, as in Adam, all die, so also in Christ shall all be made alive.

"For we know that if our earthly house of this tabernacle were dissolved, we have a building of God, an house not made with hands, eternal in the Heavens.

"For this corruptible must put on incorruption and this mortal must put on immortality. So when this corruptible shall have put on incorruption, and this mortal shall have put on immortality, then shall be brought to pass the saying that is written 'Death is swallowed up in victory. O! Death where is thy sting. O! Grave, where is thy victory. The sting of Death is sin; and the strength of sin is the law, but thanks be to God, who giveth us the victory through our Lord, Jesus Christ.' Therefore, my beloved brethren, be ye steadfast, unmovable, always abounding in the work of the Lord, for as much as ye know that your labor is not in vain in the Lord.

"Let not your heart be troubled. Ye believe in God, believe also in me. In my Father's house are many mansions. If it were not so, I would have told you, I go to prepare a place for you, and if I go and prepare a place for you, I will come again and receive you unto myself, that where I am, there ye may be also.

"The Lord is my Shepherd, I shall not want. He maketh me to lie down in green pastures. He leadeth me beside the still waters. He restoreth my soul. He leadeth me in the path of righteousness for his name's sake. Yea, though I walk through the Valley of the

Shadow of Death, I will fear no evil, for Thou art with me. Surely goodness and mercy shall follow me all the days of my life and I shall dwell in the House of the Lord forever."

PRELATE makes the following prayer, or an extemporaneous one if preferred:

"Lord of Light! in this trying hour of calamity and sorrow, we humbly lift our hearts to Thee. Give us, we pray, that light which cometh down from above. Thou hast mercifully said in Thy Holy Word that the bruised reed Thou wouldst not break; Remember in mercy, O Lord, these bereaved ones now before Thee. Be Thou at this hour, the Father of the fatherless, and the Widow's God. Administer to them the consolation which they so sorely need. Cause us to look away from this sad scene of mortality to the life which lies beyond the grave. Lead us, by Thy grace and spirit, to turn our attention to those things which make for our everlasting peace; and fix our thoughts more devotedly on Thee, the only sure refuge in time of need. And at last, when our earthly pilgrimage shall be ended, 'when the silver cord shall be loosed, and the golden bowl be broken' wilt Thou, O Father, be indeed Immanuel—God with us; may the 'lamp of Thy love' dispel the gloom of the dark valley, and we be enabled by the commendation of Thy Son to gain admission into the blessed Asylum above. Amen.

Captain General:—1. Re, 2. COVER, 3. Be, 4. SEATED.

(Choir renders appropriate music if desired.)

PRELATE:—Sir Knights, there is one sacred spot upon the earth where the footfalls of our march are unheeded; our trumpets quicken no pulse and incite no fear; the rustling of our banners and the gleam of our swords awaken no emotion. It is the silent city of the dead, to which another of our number is now to be borne, or where we now stand (if in the cemetery).

Awe rests upon every heart, and the stern warrior's eyes are bedewed with tears which never shame his manhood.

This Sir Knight was our brother. With him we have walked the pilgrimage of life and kept watch and ward in its vicissitudes and trials. He is now beyond earthly praise or censure, but we remember him in scenes which the world witnessed not, where fraternal feeling was geniune and undisguised.

His virtues linger in our memory and the recollection of his finer qualities is a consolation in this hour.

(JUNIOR WARDEN steps forward, removes sword from scabbard and presents the sword hilt foremost, over his left arm, to the Eminent Commander.)

EMINENT COMMANDER:—Our departed frater was taught that the sword in the hands of a true and courteous knight is endowed with three excellent qualities, "its hilt with justice impartial; its blade with fortitude undaunted, and its point with mercy unrestrained." He could never grasp it without being reminded of the attributes it symbolized. To this lesson, with its deep significance, we trust he gave wise heed. An inspired and heartening hope leads us to the comforting belief that he met the trying hour of dissolution with fortitude undaunted, and, waking in the dawn of the new day, received justice tempered with that mercy unrestrained which is the glorious attribute of the Son of God, and entering through the gates into the City has been admitted to the blessed companionship of just men made perfect in the realms of light and life eternal.

(COMMANDER replaces sword in scabbard or casket.)

(SENIOR WARDEN steps forward and presents a cross to the Prelate.)

PRELATE:—This symbol of the Christian's faith, hope, and trust, we again place above the breast of our frater. (done) Though the cross may, at times in the history of the world have been the badge of oppression and wrong; yet its real significance has ever remained in the heart of the Christian warrior. If an inspired apostle was not ashamed of the cross, neither should we be; if he gloried in its promise of salvation so ought we to rejoice in it as the inspiring symbol of our faith in the life beyond the grave. May this faith have been an anchor to the soul of our departed frater —may it have created in him a serene confidence in the life everlasting, a present realization of the life beyond.

Our frater was one of our mystic band, bound by fraternal ties and pledges to the noble duties,

> of feeding the hungry, clothing the naked and binding up the wounds of the afflicted,
>
> (or)
>
> of protecting innocence, relieving distress, and binding up the wounds of the afflicted.

To his friends and relatives we tender our heartfelt sympathy and affirm our faith that He who tempers the wind to the shorn lamb looks down with infinite compassion upon the widow and the fatherless in their hour of desolation; and that the same benevolent Saviour who wept tears of sympathy over the grave at Bethany, will support and comfort all those who put their trust and faith in Him.

(If the ceremony has been held in the home, chapel or Asylum, the possession will now be formed as indicated above and proceed to the cemetery. After arriving at the grave, the lines are formed as hereinbefore described and the officers and Guard of Honor at order swords, stationed as there provided. The Junior Warden then removes the sword and chapeau from the casket which will then be lowered into the grave.)

PRELATE:—"I am the resurrection and the life saith the Lord. He that believeth in me, though he were dead, yet shall he live; and whosoever liveth and believeth in me shall never die." To the earth we commit the remains of our frater, (here cast some flowers or earth on the casket), Earth to Earth, (here cast again), ashes to ashes, (here cast again), dust to dust. Delivered from the limitations of this life his soul yet liveth and abideth in the presence of the Lord Jesus Christ whose life is the judgment of our works and whose resurrection is the pledge of our immortality. Sir Knight, Farewell! God speed thee on thy heavenly way.

Let us pray:

CAPTAIN GENERAL:—1. Un, 2. COVER, (or if seated), 1. Commandery, 2. ATTENTION, 3. Un, 4. COVER.

PRELATE:—Almighty God, our heavenly Father, Author, of life and light, inspire our hearts with wisdom from on high, that we may glorify Thee in all our ways.

May we have Thy divine assistance O most merciful God! to take to heart this lesson of mortality and to labor unceasingly to redeem our misspent time. In the discharge of the important duties Thou has assigned us, may we be guided by faith and humility, courage and constancy, to the end that we may accomplish our allotted pilgrimage acceptably in Thy sight. And when our career on earth is finished, may we enter into that abundant life which Thou has assured us, through Jesus Christ our Lord, awaits Thy faithful servants in the blessed Asylum above.

COMMANDERY:—"Our Father, which art in heaven, hallowed be Thy name, Thy kingdom come. Thy will be done in earth, as it is in heaven. Give us this day our daily bread, and forgive us our debts as we forgive our debtors; and lead us not into temptation, but deliver us from evil, for Thine is the kingdom, and the power, and the glory for ever. Amen.

*Taps are sounded or chanted.

Benediction

PRELATE:—"May the grace of our Lord Jesus Christ, the love of God, and the fellowship of the Holy Ghost be and abide with us all evermore. Amen."

CAPTAIN GENERAL:— 1. Re, 2. COVER.

(The services being concluded, the Commandery is formed in column by the Captain Genral and marched to the entrance of the cemetery in silence, or at the tap of the drum.)

*(Tune: Taps)

"Frater, good-night,
Must thou go
When the day and the night
Need thee so?
All is well,
Speedeth all to their rest."

Finis.

122

INSTALLATION of OFFICERS of a COMMANDERY

The Grand Officers having been duly received and escorted to their respective stations, the Grand Commander states the purpose of the occasion, and calls upon the Grand Prelate to lead in devotional exercises. A Scripture lesson should be read, and prayer offered. If a choir is present, an appropriate selection of music may be given.

The Grand Marshal receives from the Recorder a list of the Officers elect, and retires with them to the ante room; forms them in line according to official rank—swords at a carry—Commander on right.

An altar should be placed before the Grand Commander, with Holy Bible opened, and Square, Compasses, Cross Swords, Jewels, Charter, Constitution of Grand Encampment, Statutes, and Regulations of Grand Commandery, and By-Laws of Commandery resting thereon. The Banners of the Commandery to be displayed from the Commander's station.

The Grand Marshal announces Officers-elect. The Grand Commander orders the Sir Knights to form in two divisions—swords at a carry—at open order, full width of Asylum, and inward faced.

GRAND MARCH

Grand Marshal escorts Officers-elect into Asylum, halts and faces them before Grand Commander, right resting on South. Commander is placed in center, and three paces in front of officers-elect.

The Grand Marshal will command, Present Swords! and saluting the Presiding Officer will report.

R. E. Grand Com., I present to you for installation, the Officers duly chosen.

Installing Officer:—Sir Knights, before engaging in these important ceremonies, let us unite with our Excellent Prelate in an invocation to Deity.

Carry Swords! Order Swords! Uncover! Excellent Prelate, lead our devotions.

123

(The Prelate offers an appropriate prayer ending with the Lord's Prayer, in which all join.)

Installing Officer:—Sir Knights, Recover! Carry Swords! Sir Knight Marshal, present the Commander elect.

The Grand Marshal says:

R. E. Grand Com.:—I have the honor to present to you, Sir Knight_____, who has been elected to the office of Commander of this Commandery. I find him to be well skilled in our sublime mysteries, and observant of the noble precepts of our forefathers, and have therefore, no doubt that he will discharge the important duties of his office with fidelity.

The Grand Commander then asks:—"Sir Knight are you ready to subscribe to the vow of office?" On his answering in the affirmative, the Grand Commander will draw his sword, and hold it horizontally, the edge toward the commander-elect, who will place his right hand on the blade, and uncover with his left hand.

The Grand Marshal says:—Commandery, Present Swords!

The Installing Officer says:—Repeat after me,

"I, _____, do promise and vow that I will support and maintain the Constitution, Laws and Rituals of the Grand Encampment of Knights Templar of the United States of America; and the Constitution, Laws and Regulations of the Grand Commandery of this Jurisdiction: and the By-Laws of this Commandery; and that I will faithfully discharge the duties of the office to which I have been chosen to the best of my ability?"

Grand Marshal will say:—Carry Swords! Parade Rest!

The Grand Commander will then address the Commander-elect as follows:

Eminent Com.:—Having been elected to the important and honorable station of Commander of this Commandery, it is with unfeigned pleasure that I enter upon the discharge of the duty of installing you into office. As the head of a Christian institution you are charged with important responsibilities and duties, and it is confidently anticipated that your fidelity to these trusts will reflect honor upon yourself, and credit upon your Commandery. It now becomes my duty to propose certain questions to you, to which unequivocal answers are required:

Installation

1. Do you solemnly promise, upon the honor of a Knight Templar, that you will redouble your endeavors to correct the vices, purify the morals, and promote the happiness of those of your brethren who have attained to this magnanimous Order?

2. That you will never suffer your Commandery to be opened unless there be present Nine regular Knights of the Order?

3. That you will not confer the Orders upon any one who has not shown a charitable and humane disposition, or who has not made a considerable proficiency in the preceding degrees?

4. That you will promote the general good of the Order, and on all proper occasions be ready to give and receive instructions, particularly from the Grand Officers?

5. That, to the utmost of your power you will preserve the solemnities of our ceremonies, and behave, in open Commandery, with the most profound respect and reverence, as an example to your brethren?

6. That you will not acknowledge or hold communication with any Commandery that does not work under a Constitutional Dispensation or Charter?

7. That you will not admit any Visitor into your Commandery who has not been knighted in a lawful Commandery, without his being first formally healed?

8. That you will pay due respect and obedience to the instruction of the Grand Officers, particularly relating to the several lectures and charges, and will resign the chair to them, severally, when they may visit your Commandery?

9. That you will support and maintain the Constitutions and Laws of the Grand Encampment, and the Constitution, Laws and Regulations of the Grand Commandery under whose authority you act?

10. That you will bind your successor in office to the observance of the same rules to which you have now assented?

Do you submit to all these things? And do you promise to observe and practice them faithfully?

If the Commander responds affirmatively, the Grand Commander then addresses him as follows:

Eminent Com., Having been chosen by the members of your Commandery to fill the most exalted position in their power to bestow, I congratulate you upon being the recipient of such honorable preferment, and now invest you with the jewel of your office, which is a cross surrounded by rays of light. It is to remind you that humility, love, and pure benevolence are refulgent rays that emanate from the pure and undefiled religion of the blessed Emanuel, and which should ever characterize the members of this Christian Order. It is to remind you of Him who died that He might give life to the world, and who is indeed the Lord and Saviour of all those who accept His guidance and obey His precepts.

I present you the Charter of your Commandery. You will receive it as a sacred deposit, and never permit it to be used for any other purposes than those expressed in it, and safely transmit it to your successor in office.

I also commit to your hands the Holy Bible, the great light in every degree of Masonry, together with the Cross Swords. The doctrines contained in this sacred volume create in us a belief in the existence of the Eternal Jehovah, the one only living and true God, the Creator and Judge of all things in heaven and earth; they also confirm in us a belief in the dispensations of His providence. This belief strengthens our Faith, and enables us to ascend the first step of the Grand Masonic ladder. This faith naturally produces in us a Hope of becoming partakers in the promises expressed in this inestimable gift of God to man, which Hope enables us to ascend the second step; but the third and last, being Charity, comprehends the former, and will continue to exert its influence when Faith shall be lost in sight, and Hope ends in complete fruition. The Cross Swords, resting upon the Holy Bible are to remind us that we should be "strong in the Lord and in the power of His might"; that we should put on the whole armor of God, to be able to wrestle successfully against principalities and powers, and spiritual wickedness in high places.

I also present you with the Constitution and Statutes of the Grand Encampment of the United States of America, the Constitution, Laws and Regulations of the Grand Commandery of this State, and the By-Laws of your Commandery. You will frequently consult them yourself, and cause them to be read for the information of your Commandery, that all, being informed of their duty, may have no reasonable excuse to offer for the neglect of it.

And now, Eminent Com., permit me to induct you into the chair of your Commandery, and, in behalf of the Sir Knights here assembled, to offer you my most sincere congratulations on your accession to the honorable station you now fill. It will henceforth be your special duty to preserve, inviolate, the Constitution and Laws of the Order; to dispense justice, reward merit, encourage truth and diffuse the sublime principles of universal benevolence. You will distribute alms to poor and weary pilgrims traveling from afar, feed the hungry, clothe the naked, and bind up the wounds of the afflicted. You will inculcate the duties of Charity and hospitality, and govern your Commandery with justice and moderation. And finally, my brother, may the bright examples of the illustrious heroes of former ages, whose matchless valor has shed undying lustre over the name of Knight Templar, encourage and animate you to the faithful perfomance of every duty!

Grand Marshal:—Commandery, Attention! Carry Swords! Present Swords!

Installing Officer:—Sir Knights, behold your Commander. Recollect, Sir Knights that the prosperity of your Commandery will as much depend on your support, assistance and obedience, as on the assiduity fidelity and wisdom of your Commander. Be ye therefore, diligent and faithful in the performance of your respective duties.

Grand Marshal Orders:

Sir Knights! Carry Swords! Officers-elect, Return Swords!

If the new Commander desires to offer any remarks this is the appropriate time.

Then may follow a chant or appropriate hymn by the choir.

The Grand Marshal then presents the Officers in the following words:

R. E. Grand Com.:—I have the further honor of presenting to you, for installation, these valiant Sir Knights who have been chosen to fill the various offices in this Commandery for the ensuing year, and now declare themselves ready to enter upon the duties of their respective stations.

The Grand Commander addresses the Officers-elect as follows:

Sir Knights: Before proceeding to invest you with the honor and responsibility of your respective stations, it becomes my duty to administer to you the vow of office. Do you severally consent to take upon yourselves that vow?

They bow in token of assent.

Installing Officer:—Sir Knight Grand Marshal, you will place the Officers-elect in proper position.

Grand Marshal:—Officers-elect count twos! numbers one, Draw Swords; Point Swords to left! numbers two, Grasp blade with right hand! Uncover!

Grand Marshal then says:

R. E. Grand Com.:—The Officers chosen are in proper position to take upon themselves the vow of office.

Grand Marshal, turning to the Commandery orders:—Commandery, Attention, Present, Swords!

Installing Officer:—Officers-elect, repeat after me.

VOW OF OFFICE

I, _____, do promise and vow
that I will support and maintain the Constitution,
Laws and Rituals of the Grand Encampment of
Knights Templar of the United States of America, the
Constitution, Laws and Regulations of the Grand Commandery of this jurisdiction, and the By-Laws of this
Commandery, and that I will faithfully discharge the
duties of the office to which I have been chosen, to the
best of my ability.

Grand Marshal orders:—Officers-elect, Recover.

Numbers two-Relinquish sword blade! Numbers
one—Carry swords! Return swords!

Grand Marshal addressing the Commandery,
orders:—Commandery! Carry swords! Return swords!
Be Seated.

Grand Marshal conducts the Generalissimo first,
then the remaining Officers, according to rank, to the
Altar, before the Grand Commander, introducing each
by his title, and designating the office to which he has
been chosen. The Grand Commander will receive each
of these officers with fitting words, calling attention to
their official duties and charging them to faithfulness
in discharging the same. He will also invest these
Officers with their respective jewels, and direct them
to their respective stations.

(The following are suggested as appropriate
charges:)

CHARGE TO THE GENERALISSIMO

Sir:—You have been elected Generalissimo of
this Comamndery, I now invest you with the jewel of
your office, which is a Square, surmounted by a Paschal Lamb. When beholding the Lamb, let it stimulate you to have at all times, a watchful eye over your
own conduct, and an earnest solicitude for the prosperity of the kingdom of the blessed Emanuel, the
spotless Lamb of God, who was slain from the foundation of the world.

The Square is to remind you that love and friendship should forever govern the members of Freemasonry and of the Orders of Knighthood. Your station

is on the right of your Commander; you are to assis
him in his various duties; and, in his absence, to pre
side. I charge you, therefore, to be faithful to the Si
Knights with whom you are associated; put them of
ten in remembrance of those things which tend t
their everlasting peace. Finally, "preach the word; b
instant in season, out of season; reprove, rebuke, ex
hort with all long-suffering and doctrine:" ever re
membering the promise, "Be thou faithful unto death
and I will give thee a crown of life."

CHARGE TO THE CAPTAIN GENERAL

Sir:—You have been elected Captain General o:
this Commandery. I now invest you with the jewel o:
your office, which is a Level, surmounted by a Cock
As the undaunted courage and valor of the Cock sti
mulates him to conquer his competitor, or yield him
self a victim to the contest, so should you be stimulatec
to the discharge of every duty. You should have or
"the breastplate of righteousness," so that with pa
tience and meekness you may ever travel on the leve
of humility, and be so supplied with divine grace as to
prevent you from selling your God or denying you
Master. Your station is on the left of your Command
er. Your duty, among other things, is to see tha:
due preparation is made for the various Conclaves o:
the Commandery; that the Chambers and Asylum are
in suitable array for the introduction of Candidates
and the dispatch of business. You are also to receive
and communicate to the lines all orders issued by the
Commander. You are to assist in Council, and, in the
absence of your Commander and Generalissimo, you
are to preside over the Commandery. And now, I ex
hort you, that with fidelity you perform every duty
and, "whatsoever ye do, do heartily as to the Lord, and
not unto men; continue in prayer, and watch in the
same with thanksgiving"; ever bearing in mind the
promise, "Be not weary in well-doing, for in due sea
son ye shall reap if ye faint not."

CHARGE TO THE SENIOR WARDEN

Sir:—You have been elected Senior Warden o:
this Commandery. I now invest you with the jewe

of your office, which is the Hollow Square and Sword of Justice. It is to remind you that as the children of Isreal marched in a hollow square in their journey through the wilderness, in order to guard and protect the Ark of the Covenant, so should you be vigilant in guarding every avenue from innovation and error. Let the Sword of Justice, therefore, be ever drawn to guard the Constitution of the Order. Your station is at the southwest angle of the Triangle, and upon the right of the first division. You will attend pilgrim warriors, comfort and support pilgrim penitents, and, after due trial, introduce them into the Asylum. Let it be your constant care that the warrior be not deterred from duty, nor the penitent molested on his journey. Finally, "Let your light so shine before men that they may see your good works, and glorify your Father which is in heaven."

CHARGE TO THE JUNIOR WARDEN

Sir:—You have been elected Junior Warden of this Commandery. I now invest you with the jewel of your office, which is an Eagle and Flaming Sword. It is to remind you to perform your duties with justice and valor, having an eagle eye on the prosperity of the Order. Your station is at the northwest angle of the Triangle, and on the left of the third division. Your duty is to attend weary pilgrims traveling from afar, conduct them on their journey, plead their cause, and in due time, recommend them to the Commander. You will be careful that, in addition to the pilgrim's garb, sandals, staff, and scrip, their whole preparation and deportment shall be such as to cause them to be recognized as children of humility. Teach them that "MAGNA EST VERITAS ET PRAEVALEBIT" is the motto of our Order; although they will often find the heights of fortune inaccessible, and the thorny path of life crooked, adverse, and forlorn, yet by faith and humility—courage and constancy—patience and perseverance—they may gain admission into the Asylum above, there to enjoy the rewards that await the valiant soldiers of the Lord Jesus Christ. Finally, be ye steadfast, unmovable, always abounding in the work of the Lord that you may be a shining light in the world. A city that is set on a hill cannot be hid.

CHARGE TO THE PRELATE

Sir:—You have been elected Prelate of this Commandery. I have the pleasure of investing you with this Triple Triangle, which is the jewel of your office, and a beautiful emblem of Deity. Your station is on the right of the Generalissimo. Your duty is to officiate at the Altar, and to offer up prayers to Jehovah. Your jewel is to remind you of the importance of the trust reposed in you; and may "He who is able, abundantly furnish you for every good work, preserve you from falling into error, improve strengthen, establish and perfect you," and finally greet you with "Well done, thou good and faithful servant, enter thou into the joy of the Lord."

CHARGE TO THE TREASURER

Sir:—You have been elected Treasurer of this Commandery. I now invest you with the jewel of your office which is Two Crossed Keys. Your station is on the right of the Generalissimo, in front. The qualities which should recommend a Treasurer are accuracy and fidelity—accuracy in keeping a fair and minute account of all receipts and disbursements; fidelity, in carefully preserving all the property and funds of the Commandery that may be placed in his hands, and rendering a just account of the same whenever he is called upon for that purpose. I presume that your respect and attachment to the Commandery, and your earnest solicitude for a good name, which is better that precious ointment, will prompt you to the faithful discharge of the duties of your office.

CHARGE TO THE RECORDER

Sir:—You have been elected Recorder of this Commandery. I now invest you with the jewel of your office which is Two Crossed Quill Pens. Your station is on the left of the Captain General, in front. The qualities which should recommend a Recorder are: promptitude in issuing the notifications and orders of his superior officers; punctuality in attending the Con-

:laves of the Commandery; correctness in recording :heir proceedings; judgment in discriminating between what is proper and what is improper to be committed :o writing; integrity in accounting for all moneys that may pass through his hands, and fidelity in paying the same over to the Treasurer. The possession of these good qualities, I presume has designated you for this important office, and I cannot entertain a doubt that you will discharge its duties beneficially to the Commandery and honorably to yourself. And when you shall have completed the record of your transactions here below, and finished the term of your probation, may you be admitted into the celestial Asylum of saints and angels, and find your name recorded in the Lamb's Book of Life.

CHARGE TO THE STANDARD BEARER

Sir:—You have been chosen Standard Bearer of this Commandary. I now invest you with the jewel of your office, which is a Plumb, surmounted by a Banner. Your station is in the West, and in the center of the second division. Your duty is to display, support, and protect the Banner of our Order which I now, with pleasure, confide to your valor. You will remember that it is our rallying point in time of danger; and when unfurled in a just and virtuous cause, you will never relinquish it to an enemy but with your life. Let, therefore, your conduct be such as all the virtuous will delight to imitate; let the refulgent rays, which ever emanate from pure benevolence and humility, diffuse their luster on all around that it may encourage and animate all true and courteous Knights, and, at the same time, confound and dismay all their enemies.

CHARGE TO THE SWORD BEARER

Sir:—You have been chosen Sword Bearer of this Commandery. I now invest you with the jewel of your office, which is a Triangle and Cross Swords. Your station is on the right of the Standard Bearer and on the right of the second division. Your duty is to assist in protecting the Banner of our Order, with a heart devoted to the principles of Faith, Hope and

133

Charity. Holding the mystic sword that is endowed with justice and fortitude and tempered with mercy, you may cast your eyes upon the Banner and remember that "IN HOC SIGNO VINCES" is an expressive motto of our Order, and consoling to the heart of every believer.

CHARGE TO THE WARDER

Sir:—You have been chosen Warder of this Commandery. I now invest you with the jewel of your office, which is a Square Plate with a Trumpet and Cross Swords engraved thereon. Your station is on the left of the Standard Bearer and upon the left of the second division, when separately formed. Your duty is to sound the Assembly, announce the approach and departure of the Eminent Commander, to post the Sentinels, and see that the Asylum is duly guarded. You will, also report all petitions from visitors and strangers. I charge you to be punctual in your attendance, and indefatigable in the discharge of your important duties, for though yours is among the last offices in the Commandery, it is by no means the least important.

CHARGE TO THE THREE GUARDS

Sir Knights:—You have been chosen Guards. I now invest you with the jewel of your office, which is a Square Plate with a Battle Ax engraved thereon. Your posts are those of honor as well as danger. You will, therefore, be vigilant, challenge with spirit, examine with caution, admonish with candor, relieve cheerfully, protect with fidelity, and fight valiantly.

CHARGE TO THE SENTINEL

Sir:—You have been chosen Sentinel of this Commandery, and I now invest you with the jewel of your office, which is a Square Plate with a Battle Ax engraved thereon, and this implemnt of your office. As the sword is placed in the hands of the Sentinel to enable him effectually to guard against the approach of cowans and eavesdroppers, and suffer none to pass or repass but such as are duly qualified, so it should morally serve as a constant admonition to set a guard at the entrance of our thoughts, to place a watch at the door of our lips, to post a sentinel at the avenue of our actions, thereby excluding very unqualified and unworthy thought, word and deed, and preserving consciences void of offense toward God and toward man.

As the first application from visitors for admission into the Commandery is generally made to the Sentinel at the door, your station will often present you to the observation of strangers; it is, therefore, essentially necessary that he who sustains the office with which you are entrusted, should be a man of good morals, steady habits, strict discipline, temperate, affable, and discreet. I trust that a just regard for the honor and reputation of the institution will ever induce you to inform with fidelity the trust reposed in you, and when the door of this earthly tabernacle shall be closed, may you find an abundant entrance through the gates, into the temple and city of our God.

(The presiding officer then delivers the following:)

CHARGE TO THE COMMANDERY

Sir Knights:—To manage and conduct the concerns of a Commandery of Knights Templar with that promptitude, integrity, and skill which the institution demands will require the exercise of all the talents and perserverance of its Officers and members. Are any of you solicitous that your equals and inferiors should conduct themselves toward you with deference and respect? Be sure to let no opportunity pass without furnishing them an example in your own conduct. The Officers will recollect that those moral and religious duties and precepts which they, from time to time, so forcibly impress upon the minds of others, should by no means be neglected by themselves, and the most effectual way to insure success is to let precept and example go hand in hand.

I would, therefore, exhort one and all to look well to the East, to the West, to the North, and to the South, and see that the entering avenues are strictly guarded, and that you suffer no one to pass the threshold of your Asylum but the worthy children of humility, and, at the same time, that you suffer no one to walk among you disorderly without admonition and reproof. While such is the conduct of the Officers and members, you may rest assured that this valiant, magnanimous Order will forever flourish like the green bay tree. And now, Sir Knights, I would address you in the language of David to his beloved city: "Peace be within thy walls, and prosperity within thy palaces. For my brethren and companion's sake, I will now say, Peace be within thee!

The Grand Marshal will then say:—Commandery, Attention! Draw swords! Present swords! He will then make the

OFFICIAL PROCLAMATION

Hear ye! hear ye! hear ye! Valiant Knights of the Temple! In the name of the Grand Commandery of the State of Minnesota, I hereby proclaim that the Officers of _____Commandery No._____, Knights Templar, have been duly installed into their respective stations for the ensuing Templar year, and the Commandery is now constitutionally organized for the dispatch of business. This proclamation is made to the North (one blast on trumpet), to the South (one blast), to the East (one blast), to the West (grand flourish, on trumpet). All true and courteous Knights will take due notice thereof, and govern themselves accordingly.

Grand Marshal:—Carry swords! Return swords! Be seated!

The choir may then chant the "Te Deum Laudamus," or render some other appropriate musical selection.

The Grand Commandery may then retire with a proper escort, and the Commandery will proceed with the regular order of business.

CHRONOLOGY

1. **Ancient Craft Masons.**—Add 4000 to the current year thus: A. D. 1938 plus 4000 equals 5938 A. L. (Year of Light). This refers to the Year of the Creation.

2. **Royal Arch Masons.**—Add 530 to the current year thus A. D. 1938 plus 530 equals 2468 A. I. (**Anno Inventionis**). This refers to the year of discovery.

3. **Royal and Select Masters.**—Add 1000 to the current year, thus A. D. 1938 plus 1000 equals 2938, A. Dep. (**Anno Depositionis**). This refers to the year of the deposit.

4. **Knights Templar.**—Subtract 1,118 from the current year, thus A. D. 1938 minus 1,118 equals 820, A. O. (**Anno Ordinis**). This refers to the year of the Order.

AUTHORIZATION
THE GRAND COMMANDERY, KNIGHTS
TEMPLAR of MINNESOTA.

Office of
THE GRAND COMMANDER.

Mankato, Minn., October 1, 193?

TO the KNIGHTS TEMPLAR of the STATE of
MINNESOTA:

In accordance with the authorization of The Grand
Commandery, Knights Templar of Minnesota, the fore
going Manual of Asylum Ceremonies and Tactics has
been prepared and promulgated and is hereby declared
to be the only official Manual of Asylum Ceremonies and
Tactics in effect in the State of Minnesota at the pre
sent time, superceding all other Manuals, Tactics, Floor
Plans, etc., heretofore adopted by this Grand Com
mandery, which are in conflict therewith. Its use is
mandatory in this Grand Jurisdiction.

Courteously yours,

William E. Pool

Grand Commander

MANUAL OF ASYLUM CEREMONIES

INDEX

A

Title	Page
Alarms (Warders and Sentinel's duties)	11
Approval	4
Authorization	138

B

Funeral Service	114

C

Christmas Service	103
Chronology	137

D

Definitions	6

E

Easter Service	109
Emblems and Jewels	102
Escorts of Honor	100

F

Flag presentation	75
Full Form Opening	44
Instructions	44
Reception	46
Inspection	49
Review	51
Rehearsal	48
Triangle Formation	52
Triangle Reduction	54
Alternate Formation of Triangle	62
Supplemental Full Form Opening (Dix Tactics)	65
Rehearsal of Duties	55
Full Form Opening, Red Cross	77
Funeral Ceremonies	110
Funeral Escort	112

G

General Instructions	5

H

Honors and Salutes	97

I

Insignia of Rank (Who wears)	102
Insignia of Rank (Shoulder Straps)	101
Inspection of Constituent Commanderies	56
Installation Ceremonies	123

* 9 7 8 1 9 4 1 4 7 2 9 7 2 *